HOW
AWESOME?
WILL IT BE

HOW AWESOME?
WILL IT BE

A TEENAGER'S GUIDE TO
UNDERSTANDING AND PREPARING FOR
THE SECOND COMING

ROGER A. McKENZIE

DESERET
BOOK

SALT LAKE CITY, UTAH

Library of Congress Cataloging-in-Publication Data

McKenzie, Roger (Roger A.)
    How awesome will it be? : a teenager's guide to understanding and
preparing for the Second Coming / Roger McKenzie.
        p.   cm.
    Includes bibliographical references and index.
    ISBN 1-59038-394-X (pbk.)
    1. Second Advent. 2. Church of Jesus Christ of Latter-day
Saints—Doctrines. I. Title.
    BX8643.S43.M35 2005
    236'.9—dc22
                                                              2004023074

Printed in the United States of America   54459
Malloy Lithographing, Inc., Ann Arbor, MI

10   9   8   7   6   5

To my children—Amber, Jessica, Joseph, Kaitlyn, and Michael.

To my beautiful wife, Jill, the brightest light in our family.

And to the youth, whose amazing ideas and questions enabled me to write this book.

CONTENTS

ACKNOWLEDGMENTS

In addition to expressing gratitude for the support of my family, I wish to thank Richard Ellsworth for his guidance, Chris Schoebinger for seeing something in me that I could not see in myself, and my friends at Deseret Book for their help and encouragement.

INTRODUCTION

Hope and the Second Coming

Flies. I hate flies. The nasty things are everywhere, especially during the summer. But flies are connected with the Second Coming, and I wanted my students to experience as much as they could of what the Second Coming will be like. So I drove to the store and bought five hundred plastic flies. Then I put Velcro on each one and stuck them on the walls of my seminary classroom. I put them on the TV, on ceiling fans, on pictures, on desks—everywhere! Next I put big Styrofoam balls on strings and hung them from the ceiling to represent the giant hail that would destroy the crops of the earth.

To really freak out my students, I bought a cup full of mealworms (to represent maggots, of course) to pass around the room. Finally, I made overheads of all the frightening scriptures related to the Second Coming to remind my students of the horror that was shortly to come. As I finished my preparations, I couldn't help but think about how much fun my students were going to have and about what an awesome teacher I was!

The bell rang. The time had finally come when my students would truly understand the meaning of the Second Coming! Fear and terror would run through their veins as they anticipated the signs that had been prophesied. A quiet, cynical laugh slipped from my mouth as I watched my students enter the classroom. At first they were surprised, not knowing what everything meant. But as they investigated, their curiosity turned to shock. They looked closely at the flies, commenting on how gross they were. They looked at the hail and began to question what our lesson was about. Then they saw the "maggots" and began to freak out. Just what I wanted!

The best part was when we began to read the scriptures about the events to come just prior to the Second Coming. I noticed that as we read, my students became silent. Some even slid down in their seats, their eyes as big as bowling balls. I could tell that my lesson was working and that most of the students were terrified out of their minds regarding the coming of Christ. Satisfied with what I had done, I asked for questions. My students just sat there in stunned silence. It had worked! This was a lesson they would never forget.

At that moment, one student slowly raised her hand. With a confused expression she said slowly, "What if I don't make it?"

"What do you mean?" I asked.

"Well, the things you've talked about today tell me that I'm probably not going to live through the Second Coming. What if I'm riding my bike home from school and flies begin to chase me. You said that churches would be safe places, so I race for the nearest church. But just as I bang on the front door, the flies begin to eat me. What will I do then, Brother McKenzie? I want to be saved, but you make it sound like there's no hope. What will I do?"

I stared at her for a moment, looked at the flies covering my classroom, and then turned back to her. Just then the bell rang, and the students quickly left. I was left alone, not having had an opportunity to answer her question. All the enthusiasm I had had about my Second Coming lesson was gone. My excitement about the maggots and the hail and the flies had disappeared. The scriptures we had read together faded in my mind. I went to my office and sat at my desk with one thought: *What have I done?*

Several years have passed since I gave that horrible lesson. Since then I have changed my outlook on the Second Coming. Better yet, I have changed how I teach it. No more maggots. No more hail. And definitely no more flies. That may disappoint some of you, but I listened carefully to my student that day. The one word she said that has stayed with me all these years is *hope*. And hope is what the Second Coming is all about.

As members of The Church of Jesus Christ of Latter-day Saints, we have great reason to hope for the future. One of our Articles of Faith says, "We believe all things, we hope all things, we have endured many things, and hope to be able to endure all things. If there is anything virtuous, lovely, or of good report or praiseworthy, we seek after these things" (Articles of Faith 1:13). We "hope all things" and "hope to be able to endure all things." What a great statement. Having hope regarding the Second Coming means looking forward to seeing Christ and wanting to be with him, to hear him speak, and to watch him reign with peace on earth.

The great prophet Nephi said we must "press forward with a stead-fastness in Christ, having a perfect brightness of hope" (2 Nephi 31:20). For the righteous, hope, not fear, is what helps us look forward to the Second Coming. Flies, hailstorms, and maggots shouldn't occupy our minds. Rather, we should look forward to the awesome day when Christ comes to bring peace and joy. That's what the Second Coming is all about.

When I was young, I loved Christmas. It's still one of my favorite holidays. There's food, gift giving and gift getting, more food, fun with the family, and even more food. But the best part of Christmas was my belief in Santa. I could hardly go to sleep because of the excitement I felt knowing he was on his way. At times I even thought I could see Rudolf's red nose outside my window and hear Santa walking around our living room. The excitement was almost too much for me!

I focused on the joy of Christmas, and I had hope for its arrival. I didn't waste time wondering about the possibility that Santa might hit his head on the way down our chimney and end up in a heap in our fireplace. I didn't worry about Rudolph's nose going out and Santa losing his way and slamming his reindeer into a mountainside. I looked forward to his coming with faith and hope.

The prophet Alma said, "If ye have faith ye hope for things which are not seen, which are true" (Alma 32:21). Santa always came, and he still does in one way or another as we love and serve each other and remember God's ultimate gift to us—his Son. Childlike belief and hope for the future should remain with us, especially as we look forward to the coming of Christ.

If there's only one thing you remember after reading this book, I hope it is this: Jesus lives. He is a resurrected being who knows you and wants you to have faith and hope in him. Read the testimonies of those who know him and have faith and hope in him:

> President Gordon B. Hinckley: "Jesus is the Christ, [the] immortal Son, who under His Father's direction was the Creator of the earth. He was the great Jehovah of the Old Testament, who condescended to come into the world as the Messiah, who gave His life on Calvary's cross in His wondrous Atonement because He loved us." ("Testimony," *Ensign,* May 1988, 71)

> President James E. Faust: "Mine is the certain knowledge that Jesus is our divine Savior, Redeemer, and the Son of God the Father. I know of his reality by a sure perception so sacred I cannot

give utterance to it." ("Heirs to the Kingdom of God," *Ensign*, May 1995, 63)

Elder Henry B. Eyring: "I am grateful that I know as surely as did the apostles Peter, James, and John that Jesus is the Christ, our risen Lord, and that he is our advocate with the Father." ("Witnesses for God," *Ensign*, November 1996, 33)

Elder Boyd K. Packer: "I know by experience too sacred to touch upon that God lives, that Jesus is the Christ." ("The Candle of the Lord," *Ensign*, January 1983, 56)

Joseph Smith: "And now, after the many testimonies which have been given of him, this is the testimony, last of all, which we give of him: That he lives! For we saw him, even on the right hand of God; and we heard the voice bearing record that he is the Only Begotten of the Father." (D&C 76:22–23)

Isn't it wonderful to know that so many people in our day have such strong testimonies of our Savior? Many have seen him, many see him today, and many more will see him on that incredible day when he appears in the clouds of heaven to greet us and lead the world in righteousness and love. He is our king. Jesus loves you, and he wants nothing more than for you to look to the Second Coming with hope and excitement, not fear and doubt.

He said, "Wherefore, be of good cheer, and do not fear, for I the Lord am with you, and will stand by you; and ye shall bear record of me, even Jesus Christ, that I am the Son of the living God, that I was, that I am, and that *I am to come*" (D&C 68:6; emphasis added).

He will come. As you hope for the future and put your faith in him, you will come to feel excitement for his return. It will be a day that will bring you joy and peace. No more focusing on maggots, hailstorms, and flies (although we will take a healthy look at those things later). Let's change our view from fear to hope and faith, and with greater understanding let's open our minds and hearts to the greatest day yet to come—the second coming of Jesus Christ.

PART ONE

UNDERSTANDING THE SECOND COMING

CHAPTER 1

Why Is the Second Coming So Important?

Promises, promises, promises. It seems that good friends always keep their promises. Several years ago I met a girl with whom I fell madly in love. She was beautiful, talented, and fun to be with. I finally got up enough courage to ask her out. She said yes! I couldn't believe it. I don't even remember what we did because I was so happy to be going out with her. We were together, and that's all that mattered. I was a prince in frog's clothing, and she was a beautiful princess.

We went out a few more times, and I was beginning to wonder if she liked me the way I liked her. The magic moment finally arrived. I took her to her door and was saying goodbye when she stepped close to me, took me by the hand, looked deep into my eyes, and asked, "Would you like to go to general conference with me on Saturday?" Not exactly what I expected, but of course I said yes.

There was a minor problem though. I was going to be in Idaho staying with a friend the night before conference. If I was going to go with her, I would have to leave Idaho at about three in the morning to make it back for our date—the first session of conference. I knew it would be worth it! I told her I would make it in time, and she promised to pick me up at 8:30 A.M.

As promised, I drove most of the night so I could meet her for our conference date. When I reached my home, I quickly got ready. I was tired and exhausted, but I was excited to be with her. In my best suit, with scriptures in hand, I excitedly looked out the window at 8:30 A.M.

Half an hour later I was still looking. *We have plenty of time,* I thought to myself. But by 9:30 A.M., she was still nowhere in sight. I began to worry and feel that it might be a good idea to give her a call. But then a thought crossed my mind: *I want to see if she can keep her promise to pick me up in time for conference.* It would be a great way to find out if she liked me enough to understand what I went through to meet her on time. I didn't call.

I sat down on the couch and waited until 10 A.M., staring into the distance. Another hour soon passed. My frustration turned to disappointment. Then at 11:30 A.M. the phone rang. I quickly picked it up.

"I'm sorry," she said. "My alarm didn't go off, and I slept in." I couldn't believe what I was hearing. I drove most of the morning to be with her. My mind understood that she didn't pick me up because she slept in, but my heart understood that she didn't care about me enough to keep her promise. What other promises would she not be able to keep in the future? Later we decided that it would be best not to go out anymore.

Since then I have become a little more forgiving. I've also learned that an eternal connection exists between friendship and promises. That's part of what the Second Coming is all about: God keeping his promises to his friends. The Lord said, "I will call you friends, for you are my friends, and ye shall have an inheritance with me"

(D&C 93:45). The Savior is our best friend, and he will always keep his promises to us (2 Nephi 10:17).

Elder Harold B. Lee said:

> The Lord has placed the responsibility for directing the work of gathering in the hands of the leaders of the Church to whom he will reveal his will where and when such gatherings would take place in the future. It would be well—before the frightening events concerning the *fulfillment of all God's promises* and predictions are upon us—that the Saints in every land prepare themselves and look forward to the instruction that shall come to them from the First Presidency of this Church as to where they shall be gathered and not be disturbed in their feelings until such instruction is given to them as it is revealed by the Lord to the proper authority. (In Conference Report, April 1948, 55)

Look at this list of promises the Lord has made to us regarding his coming:

- He will come again and reward us according to our works (Matthew 16:27).
- He will redeem us, and we will reign with him on the earth (D&C 43:29).
- There will be peace and no more war (Isaiah 2:4).
- If we repent, we will have no guilt when he comes (3 Nephi 27:16).
- We will become like him (D&C 132:19, 20, 23).
- We will see and hear great and marvelous things, and we will be filled with joy (3 Nephi 17:16–18).
- We will all see him together (D&C 101:23).
- Sorrow will end (D&C 101:29).
- He will reveal all things to us (D&C 101:32–33).

• We will live with him, and he will be our king and lawgiver (D&C 45:59).

Christ has promised us all this and more when he comes—if we are faithful and endure to the end. Why, then, is the Second Coming so important? Because many of the promises God has made to his children will be fulfilled when the Son returns. There will be no waiting and wondering if he will show up. The heavenly trumps will sound. He will come, and he will keep his promises. What an incredible day to look forward to.

CHAPTER 2

When Will the Savior Come?

Timing is everything. You've probably heard that phrase before, and if you think about it carefully, there's a lot of truth to it. For example, timing is everything when you're telling a joke. Blow the punch line, and the joke's not funny. Timing is essential in athletics. If your timing's off, you miss a pass or drop a handoff. Timing is crucial in cooking. Leave a hamburger on the grill too long and it becomes a chunk of charcoal. Timing is also important at home. You don't go to your mom or dad when they're in a bad mood and ask for twenty bucks and the keys to the car.

Consider the importance of timing in the following story. Audrey Mestre was a world-class free diver. Free diving is a sport in which individuals see how deep they can go underwater on just one breath of air. Without air tanks or breathing devices, divers hold tightly to a weighted sled that slides on a cable into the sea, plummeting them to record depths.

Audrey was competitive, and at twenty-eight years old she was determined to set a new world record depth of 561 feet. By comparison, the Church Office Building in Salt Lake City is 420 feet tall. Once at the bottom, Audrey would quickly fill an air bag that would speed her to the surface and fresh air. She had to hurry because she could only last about three minutes without oxygen before blacking out.

Audrey's timing, however, was off because something went terribly wrong. Bad weather on the surface caused the cable she was riding to the surface to bow. What's worse, the bag that was supposed to fill with air and shoot her to the surface didn't fully inflate. Audrey's rise to the top took much too long. After she had been under water for more than eight minutes, a rescue diver brought her body to the surface—a tragedy that would have been prevented had her timing been right (Thomas K. Grose, "Depths of Passion," *U.S. News & World Report*, 16 August 2004, 80–81).

God's timing, by contrast, is perfect. He knows all things (D&C 38:2). He knows what has happened to you in the past, what's happening to you now, and what will happen to you in the future. He also knows the answer to a question many of us have asked: When will Christ come again? (Matthew 24:36). Although no one else knows the day and the hour of the Second Coming, the scriptures help us understand a little about the timing of the Lord's return.

For example, "I come quickly," "nigh at hand," and "soon" (D&C 33:18; 43:17; 38:8) make it sound as if his second coming is close. But how close? According to D&C 110:16, his coming is "near, even at the doors." Wow! It sounds as if the Lord is on the world's doorstep and about to knock. But these verses were revealed to the Prophet Joseph Smith more than 150 years ago. So do we really know how close the Second Coming is?

Let's look at a few more scriptures that might help us. In D&C 77:6, 12, 13, we learn that the temporal earth is seven thousand years old and that the last thousand years will be the Millennium, after Christ comes. In D&C 77:12, we learn that Christ will come at the beginning of the seventh thousand years. Our calendars place the beginning of that thousand-year period at about the year 2000. So why hasn't he come yet? According to D&C 77:13, there is a time between the beginning of the seventh thousand years and the coming of Christ. How long it will be? We don't know. All we know for sure is that

- Christ will come during the seventh thousand years.
- Christ will not come right at the beginning of that period.
- There will be a period between the year 2000 and his coming.

I went to the Philippines on my mission. It's a jungle country that's hot and humid. One beautiful Sunday we decided to bring a few investigators to sacrament meeting. We introduced them to several people and took our seats so the service could begin. We then sang some great hymns that invited the Spirit. I was so excited that this might be the day that our investigators committed to be baptized.

But then the concluding speaker stood up. The first words out of his mouth were, "I have calculated when the exact month and year of the Second Coming will be." If I remember correctly, he said we could expect Christ by the year 1997. Unfortunately, our investigators never returned.

The Prophet Joseph Smith said, "Jesus Christ never did reveal to any man the precise time that He would come. Go and read the Scriptures, and you cannot find anything that specifies the exact hour He would come; and all that say so are false teachers" (*Teachings*, 341).

The Lord says, "The hour and the day no man knoweth, neither the angels in heaven, nor shall they know until he comes" (D&C 49:7). We don't know exactly when Jesus will come. All we have is pieces of information, which the Lord has been gracious enough to share with us.

God is perfect in his timing. He knows the exact moment Christ will come in glory to save the righteous and destroy the wicked. Elder Bruce R. McConkie wrote, "The time for the Second Coming of Christ is as fixed and certain as was the hour of his birth. It will not vary as much as a single second from the divine decree. He will come at the appointed time. . . . [Jesus Christ] knows the set time and so does his Father" (*The Millennial Messiah*, 26–27).

Elder Boyd K. Packer gave us some great insight into the time of Christ's coming. He said: "Teenagers also sometimes think, 'What's the use? The world will soon be blown all apart and come to an end.' That feeling comes from fear, not from faith. No one knows the hour or the day (D&C 49:7), but the end cannot come until all of the purposes of the Lord are fulfilled. Everything that I have learned from the revelations and from life convinces me that there is time and to spare for you to carefully prepare for a long life" ("To Young Women and Men," *Ensign*, May 1989, 59).

What great counsel! Prepare for a long life, and fill yourself with faith, not fear. We live at such a great time, with great things to look forward to. God knows your heart, and as you carefully live a life of faith and hope you will be ready for the coming of his Son.

CHAPTER 3

Prophets and Apostles

Several years ago I was flying over Texas from San Antonio to Wichita Falls in a small jet that seated about a dozen people. This was my first time in such a small jet, and I was excited to see and feel what it would be like to fly in it. When the plane took off, I felt my body press into the back of the seat. It felt like a ride at Disneyland.

The flight lasted only an hour, but as we approached the Wichita Falls airport, we hit some turbulence. It wasn't too bad at first, but then the plane started shaking violently. I grabbed onto my seat with a death grip born of fear and looked out my window, only to see the wing of the plane moving up and down so rapidly that I thought it would break off.

I wondered what we were going to do. At that moment a soft, calm voice came over the intercom and said, "Everything's all right. We're experiencing some turbulence, but we have everything under control and will be landing soon." I was so glad to hear the voice of the pilot. I somehow knew that he was telling the truth and that I would be all right, although I didn't immediately let go of the seat. The pilot knew the course he should take, and he guided us to where we needed to be. He had the information to keep us safe from harm.

I feel the same way about our living apostles and prophets. They have information that will guide us to safety if we will listen to them and obey their counsel. They are special witnesses of Jesus Christ to all the world (D&C 107:23). They desire to bring us closer to Christ so that we may prepare ourselves for his coming. Let's take a look at what kind of witnesses they are.

After Jesus was crucified, the apostles gathered together, wondering what to do next. As they were talking, Jesus appeared to them and said, "Behold my hands and my feet, that it is I myself: handle me, and see; for a spirit hath not flesh and bones, as ye see me have" (Luke 24:39). Each of the apostles then had the opportunity to *see for himself* that Jesus was alive again with a resurrected body.

Elder Harold B. Lee said:

> May I impose to bear my own testimony. I was visiting with one of the missionaries some years ago when two missionaries came to me with what seemed to be a very difficult question, to them. A young Methodist minister had laughed at them when they had said that apostles were necessary today in order for the true church to be upon the earth. And they said the minister said: "Do you realize that when they met to choose one to fill the vacancy caused by the death of Judas, that they said it had to be one who companied with them and had been a witness of all things pertaining to the mission and resurrection of the Lord? How can you say you have apostles, if that be the measure of an apostle?"
>
> And so these young men said, "What shall we answer?" I said to them: "Go back and ask your minister friend two questions. First, how did the Apostle Paul gain what was necessary to be

called an apostle? He didn't know the Lord; had no personal acquaintance. He hadn't accompanied the apostles. He hadn't been a witness of the ministry, nor the resurrection of the Lord. How did he gain his testimony sufficient to be an apostle? Now the second question you ask him: How does he know that all who are today apostles have not likewise received that witness?"

I bear witness to you that those who hold the apostolic calling may, and do, know of the reality of the mission of the Lord. ("Born of the Spirit," 13)

You may be asking yourself, "What does this have to do with the Second Coming?" Hang on, we'll get there. The Lord always follows a pattern of revealing himself to his apostles and prophets. He revealed himself to Adam, Enoch, Noah, and Abraham. Book of Mormon prophets Lehi, Nephi, Jacob, Mormon, Moroni, and the brother of Jared also saw him. If the Lord always follows a pattern of revealing himself to chosen witnesses, what about our apostles today?

Elder Boyd K. Packer said:

One question . . . I am asked occasionally . . . is, "Have you seen Him?" That is a question that I have never asked of another. I have not asked that question of my Brethren in the Council of the Twelve, thinking that it would be so sacred and so personal that one would have to have some special inspiration—indeed, some authorization—even to ask it.

Though I have not asked that question of others, I have heard them answer it—but *not* when they were asked. I have heard one of my Brethren declare, "I know, from experiences too sacred to relate, that Jesus is the Christ." I have heard another testify, "I know that God lives, I know that the Lord lives, and more than that, I know the Lord." (*Teach Ye Diligently,* 86)

I am so grateful for good men who can fly the gospel plane to safety. They have the kind of knowledge that will get us to our destination on time, intact, and without any white-knuckled experiences. Understanding their testimonies will help us feel safe about the coming of the Lord.

Think of all the times Christ has appeared to his chosen servants in these latter days. First, he appeared to Joseph Smith in the Sacred Grove. The First Vision took place for several reasons but primarily to restore the gospel and usher in the last days. Through Joseph Smith the Lord said, "I will suddenly come to my temple" (D&C 36:8). On April 3, 1836, the Lord appeared to Joseph Smith and Oliver Cowdery *suddenly* in the Kirtland Temple (D&C 110).

Jesus appeared to many of his servants in the past, and he visits many today. We can have faith in the apostles and prophets because they know that Christ lives and directs his Church. So as you think of the Second Coming, try not to see it as just one big event. Rather, think of it as many great events connected together to prove that Jesus keeps his promises and that there are many who witness of him. Those witnesses hold the keys and authority of the priesthood, so it's up to us to follow their counsel and guidance.

Elder Robert D. Hales told the following story:

> At the Copenhagen Denmark Area Conference held August 3–5, 1976, President [Spencer W.] Kimball went to see Thorvaldsen's beautiful sculpture[s]. . . . After a few spiritual moments admiring *The Christus*, President Kimball bore his testimony to the caretaker who stood nearby. As he turned to the statue of Peter and pointed to the large set of keys in Peter's right hand, he proclaimed: "The keys of priesthood authority which Peter held as President of the Church I now hold as President of the Church in this dispensation." Then he stated to the caretaker, "You work every day with Apostles in stone, but today you are in the presence of living Apostles." He then introduced President N. Eldon Tanner, Elder Thomas S. Monson, and Elder Boyd K.

Packer. He presented the caretaker with a Book of Mormon in Danish, and bore his testimony of the Prophet Joseph Smith. The caretaker was moved to tears in acknowledgment of the Spirit he felt in the presence of a prophet and Apostles. He acknowledged to me as we left the church, "Today I have been in the presence of servants of God." ("Examples from the Life of a Prophet," *Ensign*, November 1981, 20)

I am so grateful for the Lord's apostles and prophets. They testify and preach of Christ, and if we follow their counsel and guidance, we will approach the Second Coming not with turbulence, fear, and white knuckles but with the smooth landing of hope and peace.

President Harold B. Lee gave it to us straight when he said, "We don't need more prophets to speak—we need more ears to listen" (as quoted by A. Theodore Tuttle, in Conference Report, April 1970, 85).

CHAPTER 4

The New Jerusalem

I love traveling to new places, but the place I look forward to seeing the most is called the New Jerusalem. It's not built yet, but it will be one of the greatest cities on the face of the earth. Let's take a look at the New Jerusalem, or Zion, and see how it fits into the Second Coming.

Remember earlier how I said that God keeps all of his promises? Here is another promise he will keep. In Moses 7:62–64 the Lord promises that he will come and live with the righteous Saints in a place called the New Jerusalem. Many of us have heard of this city, but what follows is some information that will get you excited about it.

First of all, where will this new city be built? "In accord with the revelations given to the Prophet Joseph Smith, we teach that the Garden of Eden was on the American continent *located where the City Zion, or the New Jerusalem, will be built*," said Elder Alvin R. Dyer (*The Refiner's Fire*, 17–18; emphasis added).

The Lord has said that the New Jerusalem will be built in a place called Independence, Missouri (D&C 57:1–3). Now, if you have ever been to Independence, you know there really isn't much there except for some big fields and open spaces. But some day a huge city with temples will be built there. It will be a city from which the Lord will rule the world. Elder Dyer envisioned "a temple complex such as has never been known." At its center will be the great temple of the New Jerusalem in which the Lord will make his appearance, and from which he will govern all the earth ("The Center Place of Zion," 7).

Are you excited yet? This is going to be an amazing place. It will be a city built for the coming of Christ and for the Saints to come and rest from their trials and tribulations. Elder Dyer added, "For Zion, 'the New Jerusalem,' is yet to be built, and it is to be 'a land of peace, a city of refuge, a place of safety for the saints of the Most High God'" ("Center Place of Zion," 8; D&C 45:66).

There won't be any need for light in this city—no streetlights, no flashlights, no headlights on your car, no light of any kind. Elder Orson Pratt said, "Zion will not need the sun when the Lord is there, and all the city is lighted up by the glory of his presence. . . . When the people meet together in assemblies like this, in their Tabernacles, the Lord will meet with them, his glory will be upon them; a cloud will overshadow them by day and if they happen to have an evening meeting they will not need . . . lights of an artificial nature, for the Lord will be there and his glory will be upon all their assemblies. So says Isaiah the Prophet, and I believe it" (in *Journal of Discourses*, 14:355–56; D&C 88:7–13).

The New Jerusalem will be the ultimate city. The only power the city will need will come from the Savior himself. It's so hard to imagine such a great place, but it will be built. But who will build this city? We don't know when it will be constructed, but we do know something about the contractors and builders. The New Jerusalem will be built by (1) "the remnant of Jacob," (2) Gentiles who "shall come in unto the covenant and be numbered among . . . the remnant of Jacob," and

(3) "as many of the house of Israel as shall come" (3 Nephi 21:22–23; Ether 13:2–12).

And who is the remnant of Jacob? President Marion G. Romney explained, "It is certain that the believing, repentant, righteous, faithful Indians shall be among 'the remnant of Jacob' who are to build the New Jerusalem to which the Savior will come" (in Ludlow, *A Companion to Your Study of the Book of Mormon*, 281).

Can you imagine the incredible group of people that will build this great city? I can't think of a greater place where members of the Church from around the world could be working together as one. I love the phrase "If we build it, he will come." Wouldn't it be great to be building a city for the coming of the Lord? How would you feel as you poured cement, planted flowers, or made lunch for the workers? I can't imagine a happier people anywhere than those who will get to build a city in anticipation of the coming of Christ.

Here's another thing to be excited about. Do you remember the city of Enoch? Enoch worked so hard to get his people to repent that all of them finally did. His city became so righteous that it was taken into heaven. Think about eating at Taco Bell on that day! The whole thing would have been lifted up to heaven (Moses 7:13–21). Of course, for me, Taco Bell is heaven anyway. But what an incredible thing to happen! Enoch's city, the original Zion, was lifted up to God's presence. As cool as that sounds, we will probably never see that city again. Or will we?

Here's what Elder Bruce R. McConkie said about the city of Enoch and the New Jerusalem: "Enoch's city, with its translated inhabitants now in their resurrected state, shall return, as a New Jerusalem, to join with the city of the same name which has been built upon the American continent. When this earth becomes a celestial sphere 'that great city, the holy Jerusalem,' shall again descend 'out of heaven from

God,' as this earth becomes the abode of celestial beings forever" (*Doctrinal New Testament Commentary*, 3:581).

I can't wait for the opportunity to see that happen! One city will be built on earth for the coming of Christ and the other will descend from heaven to join it and all the righteous Saints. The tenth article of faith states that the New Jerusalem will be built and Christ will reign personally upon the earth. The New Jerusalem will be the capital city for the righteous—a city where promises will be fulfilled and where we can find peace and rest.

It will be an incredible time when people march together to the New Jerusalem. Orson Pratt said:

> We shall go back to Jackson County. Not that all this people will leave these mountains, or all be gathered together in a camp, but when we go back there will be a very large organization consisting of thousands, and tens of thousands, and they will march forward, the glory of God overshadowing their camp by day in the form of a cloud, and a pillar of flaming fire by night, the Lord's voice being uttered forth before his army.
>
> Such a period will come in the history of this people, and when it arrives the mountains and the hills will be ready to break forth with a loud voice before the Lord's army, and the very trees of the field will wave to and fro by the power of God, and clap like hands. The everlasting hills will rejoice. . . . Will not this produce terror upon all the nations of the earth? Will not armies of this description, though they may not be as numerous as the armies of the world, cause a terror to fall upon the nations?
>
> The Lord says the banners of Zion shall be terrible. . . . When the Lord's presence is there, when his voice is heard, and his angels go before the camp, it will be telegraphed to the uttermost parts of the earth and fear will seize upon all people, especially the

wicked, and the knees of the ungodly will tremble in that day. (In *Journal of Discourses*, 15:364)

How would you like to be part of that army? What an awesome experience it will be to see people march forth with the power of God to build his city. Imagine the day when leaders of the Church say, "Pack your bags! We're going to build the New Jerusalem!"

CHAPTER 5

Adam-ondi-Ahman

Deacons are cool. Think about the deacons in your ward for just a moment. Every week you get an opportunity to partake of the sacrament because of them. I love to watch them walk to their assigned spots and begin to pass the sacrament to those of us in the congregation. But every now and then I have to laugh a little.

Here are a bunch of boys who just graduated from Primary, where they sang Primary songs and learned about the basics of the gospel. Then, all of a sudden, they're transformed into Aaronic Priesthood holders, passing the emblems of the body and blood of Christ. All right, maybe the change doesn't happen overnight. Nevertheless, they're young and they're doing what the Lord has asked them to do, and that's cool!

This chapter is about the future responsibility that some deacons may have. Sisters, don't think you'll be left out. It's about you too. It's about an event such as the world has never known. It will be one of the biggest sacrament meetings ever to be held in the history of the Church, and it will take place before the Second Coming at a place called Adam-ondi-Ahman. Many members of our Church have been patiently waiting for this special day to come, so let's take a look at Adam-ondi-Ahman and get excited about the greatest gathering of Saints of all time.

Let's start with the meaning of the name *Adam-ondi Ahman*. You can probably recognize that it has something to do with Adam, but what does the rest of the name mean?

Elder Bruce R. McConkie explained: "Ahman is one of the names by which God was known to Adam. Adam-ondi-Ahman, a name carried over from the pure Adamic language into English, is one for which we have not been given a revealed, literal translation. As near as we can judge—and this view comes down from the early brethren who associated with the Prophet Joseph Smith, who was the first one to use the name in this dispensation—*Adam-ondi-Ahman means the place or land of God where Adam dwelt*" (*Mormon Doctrine*, 19–20).

It was the place where Adam and Eve lived when they were expelled from the Garden of Eden. They had to live somewhere, so they took a short journey to a place where they could live and have a family. So where exactly was Adam's first mortal home? Some people think it was somewhere in the Middle East, but the Prophet Joseph Smith said, "Adam-ondi-Ahman is located immediately on the north side of Grand River, in Daviess County, Missouri, about twenty-five miles north of Far West. It is situated on an elevated spot of ground, which renders the place as healthful as any part of the United States, and overlooking the river and the country round about, it is certainly a beautiful location" (*History of the Church*, 3:39).

You may have visited the area. Today it's farmland. There aren't any massive church buildings—no tabernacle and no conference center. It's just a quiet place where you could go to have a picnic. But about three years before Adam died, he called his children together at this place. Then he gave a farewell speech to his children and blessed them (Smith, *Doctrines of Salvation*, 3:74). It must have been a memorable time for all who were there. Daniel, a righteous hero in the Old Testament, prophesied that a similar meeting would again take place before the Second Coming (Daniel 7:9–14, 21–22, 26–27).

So has that second meeting happened already? Not yet. In fact, you may even be invited to attend. Then again, you may not even know when it occurs. President Joseph Fielding Smith gave us some information about this special meeting. He said, "When this gathering is held, the world will not know of it; the members of the Church at large will not know of it, yet it shall be preparatory to the coming in the clouds of glory of our Savior Jesus Christ as the Prophet Joseph Smith has said. The world cannot know of it. The Saints cannot know of it— *except those who officially shall be called into this council*—for it shall precede the coming of Jesus Christ as a thief in the night, unbeknown to all the world" (*The Way to Perfection*, 291; emphasis added).

That quote raises an interesting point. Who will be there? The scriptures give us the invitation list. The Lord tells us who is invited: Adam, Abraham, Isaac, Jacob, Joseph, Elijah, Elias, Peter, James, John, John the Baptist, and Moroni (D&C 27:5–14). Wow! Can you imagine seeing all of those great leaders seated on the stand! The Lord will also invite another group: "all those whom my Father hath given me out of the world" (D&C 27:14). Who are they?

Being given to the Savior "connotes an act of covenant making. To be out of the world is to fully observe and keep one's covenants with the Lord. In other words, every Latter-day Saint has the potential opportunity to meet with the Savior in a sacrament meeting experience at the time of His coming" (Otten, *Sacred Truths*, 129).

That means that every prophet of every dispensation will be there, including Lehi, Nephi, Jacob, Abinadi, Alma, Mormon, Joseph Smith,

Brigham Young, and Gordon B. Hinckley. Even you and I could be there, provided we live worthily and keep our covenants. Elder McConkie said, "Every faithful person in the whole history of the world, every person who has so lived *as to merit eternal life in the kingdom of the Father will be in attendance* and will partake, with the Lord, of the sacrament" (*The Promised Messiah*, 595).

How would you like to be a deacon at that sacrament meeting? When I was a deacon, we were assigned numbers that told us where we were supposed to pass the sacrament. If you were assigned number one, you passed to those on the stand who presided over the meeting. What if you got number one at the Adam-ondi-Ahman sacrament meeting? You would slowly walk up to the stand and pass the sacrament to the person presiding—Jesus Christ! Then you would pass the sacrament to Adam, Noah, Lehi, Moroni, President Hinckley, and all of those who have been prophets. I don't think I could do it. I would want to stop and shake hands with each of them.

Can you imagine who the speakers will be? Maybe Adam will be asked to conduct the meeting. He might say something like this, "Welcome to our sacrament service today. We will start by singing 'We Thank Thee, O God, for a Prophet,' after which Nephi will give our opening prayer." Maybe we will sing "I Know That My Redeemer Lives" as we look at the Savior himself. Jesus Christ may be the concluding speaker as he prepares the righteous for the time he comes in his glory to the earth.

Elder Bruce R. McConkie described the gathering as "the greatest congregation of faithful saints ever assembled on planet earth. It will be a sacrament meeting. It will be a day of judgment for the faithful of all the ages" (*The Millennial Messiah*, 579).

I really want to be there. I know you want to be there too. So later on I'll discuss how we can prepare for that day. What else will happen at this meeting? President Joseph Fielding Smith said, "Christ will come, and Adam will make his report. At this council Christ will be received and acknowledged as the rightful ruler of the earth. Satan will be replaced" (*Doctrines of Salvation*, 3:13).

What a great time to live. What an exciting opportunity we have as we look forward to the ultimate sacrament service of all time.

CHAPTER 6

Armageddon and the Mount of Olives

Armageddon. The name alone conjures up images of destruction, chaos, warfare, and earth-destroying comets. Books have been written and movies have been made with the same title. But books and movies have no real similarity to what Armageddon will really be. Let's get an accurate idea of what Armageddon is all about.

The Army

Many prophets in the scriptures have prophesied of a great day of destruction. Joel, Zephaniah, Zechariah, and even John the Revelator all saw the last days and told of a time that would come when all nations of the earth would be at war. They also prophesied that the focal point of the conflict would be the city of Jerusalem and the surrounding area (Zechariah 11–13; Revelation 16:14–21).

Like a swarming cloud of locusts, an army will descend on Jerusalem. Nothing will be able to stop it, and it will devour everything in its path. This massive army will number two hundred million soldiers, the biggest army ever assembled in the history of the world! Satan will be its leader, and his mission will be the destruction of the Jews (Revelation 9:8–9, 16; Joel 2:2).

Elder Bruce R. McConkie, referring to the imagery of John and Joel, suggested that "it is not improbable that these ancient prophets were seeing such things as men wearing or protected by strong armor; as troops of cavalry and companies of tanks and flame throwers; as airplanes and airborne missiles which explode, fire shells and drop bombs; and even other weapons yet to be devised in an age when warfare is the desire and love of wicked men" (*Doctrinal New Testament Commentary*, 3:503).

Satan's army will kill thousands, leaving many to wonder whether all will be lost to this indestructible force. And yet you and I know that God is much more powerful than Satan and that through small and simple things great things come to pass (1 Nephi 16:29).

Two Prophets

During this period of destruction, when Jerusalem is about to be destroyed, God will send two of his prophets to prophesy and protect the city. Elder McConkie wrote, "No doubt they will be members of the Council of the Twelve or of the First Presidency of the Church (*Doctrinal New Testament Commentary*, 3:509). Two against two hundred million! How can it be possible that these great men will defend Jerusalem against such a massive army?

"They shall have power like Elijah who called down fire from heaven to consume his enemies, and who sealed the heavens that it rained not in all Israel for the space of three and a half years (1 Kings 17–18; 2 Kings 1), and like Moses, by whose word blood and plagues lay heavily upon the Egyptians" (*Doctrinal New Testament Commentary*, 3:510).

Their incredible powers will prevent Jerusalem from being

destroyed. The great prophet Isaiah said they shall be "full of the fury of the Lord" (Isaiah 51:20). How would you like to watch that on television?

For three and a half years, these prophets will protect the city with great miracles. They will be Israel's only hope, but this hope will not last. Eventually these prophets will be captured by the army of darkness and killed. Their bodies will be left in the streets of Jerusalem for three and a half days as the army of evil celebrates and plunders the city (Revelation 11:2, 7–9).

"And they that dwell upon the earth shall rejoice over them, and make merry, and shall send gifts one to another; because these two prophets tormented them that dwelt on the earth" (Revelation 11:10).

The gift giving among the wicked, however, will prove premature. God always has a way of surprising the wicked just when they think they have him beat. After the prophets have lain dead in the streets for all to see, a great voice from heaven will say, "Come up hither!" Then, as everyone watches, even the army of Satan, these two powerful prophets will be resurrected. They will stand on their feet and rise to heaven. Fear will overcome their enemies, and it will be time for them to return their gifts! (Revelation 11:11–12).

The Mount of Olives

During the siege of Jerusalem, when all hope seems lost, "when the hostile troops of several nations are ravaging the city and all the horrors of war are overwhelming the people of Jerusalem, [Jesus] will set his feet upon the Mount of Olives, which will cleave and part asunder at his touch" (Charles W. Penrose, "The Second Advent," *Millennial Star*, 21: 583; Zechariah 14:4–5).

After the Jews flee to safety through the cleft in the Mount of Olives, they will look upon their deliverer and ask, "What are these wounds in thine hands and in thy feet?" When they realize that Jesus is their Messiah, they will weep because they persecuted their king (D&C 45:51–53). Their doubts will then depart, and they will become converted to the Lord.

Soon after these events, Elder Joseph Fielding Smith said, the Lord will "come out of His hiding place" and will unleash his fury on the wicked (*Signs of the Times*, 170). He will send plagues on the army of evil, causing their flesh to rot and sores to cover their skin (Zechariah 14:12; Revelation 16:2–11). Yuck!

He will send a hailstorm that will destroy them and their weapons of war. John the Revelator said the hailstones will be about the weight of a talent—75.6 pounds! (Revelation 16:21; Bible Dictionary, 789). A bowling ball weighs sixteen pounds. Can you imagine 75-pound hail flying out of heaven? Run! But there's more.

An earthquake "such as was not since men were upon the earth" will shake the world. Earth's land masses will come together, and islands and continents will become one land. Members of the massive army will turn against each other as destruction befalls them; only one-sixth of the army will survive. Death and destruction will be so severe among the wicked that it will take seven months to bury the dead (Revelation 16:18; D&C 133:21–24; Ezekiel 38:21; 39:2, 11–16; Zechariah 14:13).

President Joseph Fielding Smith said:

> I know these are unpleasant things. It is not a pleasant thing even for me to stand here and tell you that this is written in the Scriptures. If the Lord has a controversy with the nations, He will put them to the sword. Their bodies shall lie unburied like dung upon the earth. That is not nice, is it, but should we not know it? Is it not our duty to read these things and understand them? Don't you think the Lord has given us these things that we might know and we might prepare ourselves through humility, through repentance, through faith, that we might escape from these dreadful conditions that are portrayed by these ancient prophets? That is

why I am reading them. I feel just as keenly as you do about the condition, and I pray for it to come to an end, but I want it to come to an end right. . . .

So I pray every day of my life that the Lord will hasten His work; and while all this has to take place, I hope He will hasten it, that it may soon come to an end, that peace may come; and so I repeat, as I said in one of the talks sometime ago, I am praying for the end of the world because I want a better world. I want the coming of Christ. I want the reign of peace. I want the time to come when every man can live in peace and in the spirit of faith, humility and prayer. (*Signs of the Times,* 154–55, 175)

The battle of Armageddon and Christ's appearance at the Mount of Olives will happen before the Second Coming. But we should not be afraid of the Savior's return, for he will destroy wickedness and bring peace. The world will be a better place for you and me. I think we should join President Smith and pray for that day to come.

CHAPTER 7

To the World

All of the events discussed to this point aren't usually considered as *the* Second Coming, but they are definitely part of the process. This chapter will cover what most of us consider the actual Second Coming—when Christ comes to the earth in power and glory.

When I was young I learned the importance of dressing appropriately for certain occasions. I would have been satisfied going to high school in my pajamas, but my parents taught me that I needed to wear certain things at certain times. For instance, going to church required the best clothes I had in order to show respect to the Lord in his house. I even discovered that going on dates required proper attire—jeans for a casual date, dress clothes for a fireside, a tuxedo for the prom.

Jesus is a great example of appropriateness. Consider the following. In Mathew 21 the Lord asked his disciples to find a donkey, which Jesus then rode into Jerusalem. Seeing him come, a huge group of people spread clothing in front of him as a sign of respect that only a king deserved. Then they cut down palm branches and waved them, shouting praises to his name.

Everything Christ does is for a reason. His actions have a special meaning or purpose. Riding into a city on a donkey symbolized peace, the clothing symbolized that he is a king, and the palm branches stood for victory and triumph. Everything that happened on that special occasion testified that Jesus Christ is the Savior of the world. His triumphal entry is a sign or type of a future triumphal entry when all the world will see him return.

At a future time, just as in the past, Jesus will come to prove to the world that he is the Messiah. But how will he look when he comes? Will he ride on a donkey to represent peace? No. Just as coming appropriately dressed to Church or to a prom is important, so Christ will come appropriately dressed for the Second Coming. Many people believe that he will probably dress as he did when he rode into Jerusalem—in a white robe. But the Second Coming is something special. Christ will be dressed in red apparel, symbolic of his taking upon himself the sins of the world. His clothing will symbolize the Atonement and the blood he shed for all mankind.

> And it shall be said: Who is this that cometh down from God in heaven with dyed garments; yea, from the regions which are not known, clothed in his glorious apparel, traveling in the greatness of his strength? . . .
>
> And the Lord shall be red in his apparel, and his garments like him that treadeth in the wine-vat. . . . And his voice shall be heard: I have trodden the wine-press alone, and have brought judgment upon all people; and none were with me;
>
> And I have trampled them in my fury, and I did tread upon them in mine anger, and their blood have I sprinkled upon my garments, and stained all my raiment; for this was the day of vengeance which was in my heart. (D&C 133:46, 48, 50–51)

Sounds pretty scary, but remember that he will be enacting vengeance upon those who have rejected him. The prophet Isaiah said Christ will come as a "great light" and as a "burning" (Isaiah 9:2, 5). Cleansing and destruction by fire will be part of his coming in glory.

Joseph Smith said Christ will come from the East (*Teachings*, 287). Just as the sun rises in the East, warms us, and keeps us alive, so Christ will come from the East and bring with him the warmth of salvation and eternal life. His arrival will not be some secret meeting like that at Adam-ondi-Ahman. The Lord said, "And *all* flesh shall see me together" (D&C 101:23; emphasis added). We will all have the opportunity to see him when he comes.

John the Revelator told us that Jesus would come on a white horse (Revelation 19:11–16). But remember that John often used symbolism. The white horse could represent Christ's coming in power and authority as a king to destroy all evil. What a wonderful image!

Elder Charles W. Penrose sums up what will happen when Christ returns:

> He comes! The earth shakes, and the tall mountains tremble; the mighty deep rolls back to the north as in fear, and the rent skies glow like molten brass. He comes! The dead Saints burst forth from their tombs, and 'those who are alive and remain' are 'caught up' with them to meet him [1 Thessalonians 4:17]. The ungodly rush to hide themselves from his presence, and call upon the quivering rocks to cover them. He comes! with all the hosts of the righteous glorified. The breath of his lips strikes death to the wicked. His glory is a consuming fire. The proud and rebellious are as stubble; they are burned and 'left neither root nor branch' [Malachi 4:1]. He sweeps the earth 'as with the besom [broom] of destruction' [Isaiah 14:23]. He deluges the earth with the fiery floods of his wrath, and the filthiness and abominations of the world are consumed. Satan and his dark hosts are taken and

bound—the prince of the power of the air has lost his dominion, for He whose right it is to reign has come, and "the kingdoms of this world have become the kingdoms of our Lord and of his Christ." ("The Second Advent," *Millennial Star,* 21: 583)

We look forward to the Second Coming with either hope or dread, depending on whether we had good seminary teachers who taught the peace of the Lord or crummy seminary teachers who taught about scary maggots and stuff.

I promise you that if you are living righteously and doing your best to live the commandments of the Lord, this will be a great day for you—not a day to fear. You will remember his love on this day. Elder Neal A. Maxwell said:

> I pause to interject a few thoughts from section 133 of the Doctrine and Covenants. It speaks of Jesus' second coming, of the dramatic solar display that will happen to the sun and the moon. Then it says, "And the stars shall be hurled from their places" (v. 49). The voice of Jesus will be heard as he speaks of having trod the winepress alone (v. 50). Then, in what seems to me to be a precious perspective, he goes on to say that we will remember his loving kindness forever and ever (v. 52). Though stars are hurled from their places, what we will remember most from that occasion is his loving kindness! ("Teaching by the Spirit," 2)

His loving kindness is what we need to remember.

PART TWO

THE SIGNS OF THE SECOND COMING

CHAPTER 8

The Purpose of Signs

I'll never forget a vacation my family and I took to Alaska. We had a great time as we explored many areas of that incredible state. It was winter, and we saw many things that people aren't able to see when they visit in the summer. One day we decided to go to a place called Portage.

Portage is a glacier that has a lake at its base, where we parked our car. Over the years many large icebergs have broken off the glacier and floated to the middle of the lake. Because the lake was frozen during our visit, we decided to walk out on it so we could explore a huge iceberg—the biggest ice cube I'd ever seen!

We climbed on as much of the iceberg as we could, took pictures, and began our walk back to the car. As we approached our car, we noticed a sign we hadn't seen before. In big letters it read:

WARNING! STAY OFF THE ICE AND AWAY FROM
THE ICEBERG. THE ICEBERG MAY FLIP AT ANY TIME!

We laughed at first, wondering how we hadn't seen the sign on our way out to the iceberg. Later we had a chance to speak with a ranger who said that a few years earlier a man had been out on the same iceberg when it flipped and killed him. We weren't laughing anymore. I wondered how we could have been so stupid as to not notice the sign the first time we walked past it.

Warning signs and messages are all around us. We see them on roads and highways, on medication bottles, and on video games. The funniest warning I ever saw was on the label of a bathroom spray can. It said, "Keep Away from Teenagers!" Signs are good for us because they make us aware of danger. That's one of the reasons we have signs of the Second Coming. If we heed signs that warn us of Christ's coming, we will have nothing to fear because we will be spiritually safe.

A second purpose for signs is to inspire us to take action and prepare for what's coming. Several years ago I had a student who was especially excited to get her driver's license. Her parents bought her an old car, finally giving her the freedom she had dreamed of. For months she told me how fun and thrilling it was to drive her own car.

One day near the end of the school year, I asked her how she was doing. For the first time, she seemed unhappy and somewhat frustrated. She told me that the oil light had come on in her car several months before. Because she didn't know what the warning light meant, she ignored it even though it stayed on. As a result, the engine in her car eventually froze up. The fun and freedom she had once enjoyed were gone. If she had taken action and heeded the warning light, she would have saved herself a lot of unhappiness.

We must heed warning signs, but we don't want to go too far. In responding to signs of the Second Coming, for example, we might focus on just one thing, such as food storage. We might buy so much food storage that we go into debt. That's a bad thing. Elder Neal A. Maxwell said, "Over the sweep of Christian history, some believers have, by focusing on a few prophecies while neglecting others, prematurely expected the Second Coming. . . . Members of the Church need not and should not be alarmists. They need not be deflected from quietly and righteously pursuing their daily lives" ("'For I Will Lead You Along,'" *Ensign*, May 1988, 7, 9). We should be looking for signs of the Second Coming, but the Lord expects us to balance our response to those signs with righteous living.

A third reason signs are important is that they help us look forward to the coming of Christ. They give us hope, as discussed earlier. Even frightening signs are evidence that the coming of Christ and the peace he will bring are getting closer. Think about how signs help us look forward to events. Reflect, for example, on the last few months of the school year. What begins to happen? Days get warmer, birds start singing, flowers begin blossoming, and everyone comes down with spring fever and wants to be outside. Summer is on its way, and with summer comes the end of the school year and freedom—at least for a few months.

So it is with the signs of the Second Coming. The righteous look forward to the signs because they indicate that the coming of the Savior is near. We should all look forward to a day of no more temptation and no more war—just peace and happiness. So instead of seeing signs as a reason to be frightened, see them as a reason to rejoice that we are getting closer to our destination.

But here's a word of caution about signs. We must listen to the right sources when it comes to interpreting the signs around us. Our friends may tell us that there is no hope because of all the terrible things that are happening. Strangers on the news may predict things to come and tell us what we should or shouldn't do. But the people we should listen to the most are the prophets and apostles. Elder Boyd K. Packer said, "The Brethren, by virtue of traveling constantly everywhere on earth, certainly know what is going on, and by virtue of prophetic insight are able to read the signs of the times. . . . Come away from any others. Follow your leaders, who have been duly ordained and have been publicly sustained, and you will not be led astray" ("'To Be Learned Is Good If . . .'" *Ensign*, November 1992, 73).

If we will trust the Brethren, we can develop greater faith. Remember what happened in the year 2000? Companies paid thousands of dollars to protect their computers from crashing on midnight of the last day of 1999. It's easy to get caught up in the confusion of whom to listen to and whom to trust.

President James E. Faust said: "Today many people are obsessed with the Y2K problem and worry about the date coming up right because of the way computers measure time. . . . While some glitches may occur, I am optimistic that no great catastrophic computer breakdown will disrupt society as we move into the next century. I have a far greater fear of the disruption of the traditional values of society ("This Is Our Day," *Ensign*, May 1999, 17).

Listen to our leaders. They will help you look for the signs, and they will explain them to you. So as you read about the signs of the Second Coming in the next few chapters, remember why signs are given:

- They *warn* us and protect us from danger.
- They *motivate* us to prepare for the future.
- They *inspire* us to look forward to the coming of Christ.

CHAPTER 9

Wars and Rumors of Wars

When I decided to join the military, I searched all of the different branches and chose what I thought would be the best one for me, the United States Air Force. It was 1991, and Desert Storm was coming to an end. One of the things I remember most about my training was preparing for chemical warfare. We began our training with a short briefing regarding how to put on gas masks. The last part of the briefing worried me the most. We learned that we were to actually experience, to a small degree, what it would be like to be in a chemical warfare environment.

We boarded a bus that drove us out to an old trailer in the middle of nowhere. About twenty of us got out of the bus and were instructed that the trailer was filled with a small amount of a chemical used in war. We put on our gas masks and, with great anxiety, entered the trailer. A small amount of mist hanging in the air made me nervous. I did not want to feel the effects of the gas. In a loud voice that echoed from under his mask, our leader yelled, "I'm going to stand in front of each one of you, and I want you to take your mask off and tell me your name and Social Security number. Then I want you to put your mask back on and go outside."

I was terrified. I stood about halfway down the line and watched as he came to each soldier. They did as he asked and then quickly ran out of the trailer.

It was my turn. He stood in front of me. I quickly took off my mask and began to state my name and number. I stuttered as I spoke my name and could hardly remember my number. My lungs began to burn, my eyes watered, and my face began to sting. I quickly put on my mask, ran from the trailer, and yanked off the mask so I could breathe the gas out of my lungs. It was a frightening experience. As I cleaned that small dose out my lungs, I thought how horrible that chemical would have been at full strength. Wouldn't it be nice not to have to worry about training like that?

Today, years later, I find myself thinking about the following scripture regarding the last days: "And in that day shall be heard of wars and rumors of wars, and the whole earth shall be in commotion, and men's hearts shall fail them" (D&C 45:26). War is a horrible thing. People die and suffer, and nations are ravaged. Why, then, is war a sign of the second coming of the Savior? Because Satan loves war. He loves suffering and will do anything to make us miserable. Let's look at a scripture that describes how Satan feels: "And he [Satan] had a great chain in his hand, and it veiled the whole face of the earth with darkness; and he looked up and laughed, and his angels rejoiced" (Moses 7:26).

God, on the other hand, wants us to choose happiness and live righteously. "Men are, that they might have joy" (2 Nephi 2:25). God knows, however, that men and women may use their agency for good or for evil, to follow him or to follow Satan. When President Gordon B. Hinckley was a member of the Quorum of the Twelve Apostles, he said:

War I hate with all its mocking panoply [display]. It is a grim and living testimony that Satan, the father of lies, the enemy of God, lives. War is earth's greatest cause of human misery. It is the destroyer of life, the promoter of hate, the waster of treasure. It is man's costliest folly, his most tragic misadventure. . . .

But since the day that Cain slew Abel, there has been contention among men. There have always been, and until the Prince of Peace comes to reign, there always will be tyrants and bullies, empire builders, slave seekers, and despots who would destroy every shred of human liberty if they were not opposed by force of arms. ("Lest We Forget," 3)

So if war is to be a part of our lives in the last days, what are we to do? The Lord says, "Renounce war and proclaim peace" (D&C 98:16). One of our responsibilities is to proclaim peace. And our responsibility to do that doesn't start with nations, it starts in our homes. We must fight Satan on our own turf. We must love and honor our parents, help and serve our brothers and sisters, and eliminate contention in our homes and schools. Then, if we are called to fight bigger worldwide battles, at least our souls will be ready. We will be at peace.

President Hugh B. Brown spoke words of comfort and assurance: "I want to say to you, brethren, that in the midst of all the troubles, the uncertainties, the tumult and chaos through which the world is passing, almost unnoticed by the majority of the people of the world, there has been set up a kingdom, a kingdom over which God the Father presides, and Jesus the Christ is the King. That kingdom is rolling forward, as I say, partly unnoticed, but it is rolling forward with a power and a force that will stop the enemy in its tracks while some of you live" ("The Kingdom Is Rolling Forth," *Improvement Era*, December 1967, 93).

Many of you are fighting this battle already. God bless you as you do your best to proclaim peace at home and at school. Captain Moroni was in a situation similar to ours today. He was a man of peace but was compelled to go to battle in order to protect his family and his beliefs. His heart did not glory in war or in killing people but "in doing good, in preserving his people, yea, in keeping the commandments of God, yea, and resisting iniquity" (Alma 48:16).

Regarding the horrible attacks on the United States on September 11, 2001, President Hinckley said, "The God in whom I believe does not foster this kind of action. He is a God of mercy. He is a God of love. He is a God of peace and reassurance, and I look to Him in times such as this as a comfort and a source of strength" ("The Times in Which We Live," *Ensign*, November 2001, 73).

As wars rage around us and all over the world, may we have the faith to believe that all things are in God's hands. May we look past the horrors of war to the glory of Christ's coming. May we look to God for strength and do as Captain Moroni did—live righteous lives so that the very powers of hell may be shaken forever (Alma 48:17).

CHAPTER 10

Fear and Despair, Faith and Peace

In the last days, the scriptures say, "Men's hearts shall fail them; for fear shall come upon all people" (D&C 88:91; Luke 21:26).

Fear can come without warning, at a moment we least expect. With a clammy grip, it slowly takes hold of its victim. Fear hisses words of discouragement such as "Give up now" and "There's no hope." As it tightens its hold, people begin to lose faith in the future. When fear injects the chilling venom of doubt, the body, once full of life and hope, becomes limp, ready to be devoured.

What a frightening definition of fear. Who wrote that anyway? Oh yeah, I did. But it does make you think about what fear can do to us. One of the prophecies of the last days is that fear will be everywhere and that there will be "weeping and wailing among the hosts of men" (D&C 29:15). Fear is exactly what Satan wants us to experience. Fear can cause even the best of us to tremble and lose strength.

What makes us fearful? First, it's the unknown—being in a situation where we don't know what the next step may bring. That's the kind of fear we experience on a thrill ride at an amusement park. We hop in the seat, the safety bar closes around us, and our hearts beat faster and faster as we anticipate the unexpected thrill of the ride. If we don't know what to expect before and during the Second Coming, we'll likely be afraid. And even if we know the signs of Christ's coming, we may still be fearful, not knowing exactly what the experience will be like. Do you remember the purpose of these signs? It's not to create fear among the righteous but to show that Christ's coming is near and that we should be preparing for that day.

Another reason we fear is that we don't understand. Sometimes we think we need to understand everything God is doing in order to have faith. That's simply not true. I'm sure Nephi was afraid when he returned to Jerusalem for the brass plates. At the time he didn't completely understand what God was going to do or what would happen. Signs of the Second Coming may be confusing, but we need to be like Nephi, who said, "And I was led by the Spirit, not knowing beforehand the things which I should do" (1 Nephi 4:6). Nephi showed God that he trusted in him and that he would "go and do" wherever or whatever God asked of him (1 Nephi 3:7).

The third reason people fear, and this may be especially true when Christ comes, is sin. Sin can destroy our faith in God, decrease our ability to listen to the promptings of the Spirit, and weaken our desire to endure to the end. Remember in the Book of Mormon when the final battle was about to take place between the Nephites and the Lamanites? Let's read how Mormon described the situation:

"And it came to pass that my people, with their wives and their children, did now behold the armies of the Lamanites marching towards them; and with that awful fear of death which fills the breasts of all the wicked, did they await to receive them. . . . And every soul was filled with terror" (Mormon 6:7–8). The fear caused by sin will eventually destroy us—just as it did the Nephites—if we do not change.

Another prophecy about the last days and the righteous has nothing to do with fear. It's all about peace, faith, and a righteous city. Do you remember the New Jerusalem? The scriptures call it "a land of *peace,* a city of *refuge,* a place of *safety* for the saints of the Most High God; and the glory of the Lord shall be there, and the terror of the Lord also shall be there, insomuch that the wicked will not come unto it, and it shall be called Zion. . . . And it shall come to pass that the righteous shall be gathered out from among all nations, and shall come to Zion, singing with songs of everlasting joy" (D&C 45:66–67, 71; emphasis added). It will be a day of fear and doubt for the wicked but a day of peace and increased faith for the righteous.

Do you remember when you heard about the attack on the Twin Towers in New York on September 11, 2001? How did you feel? What did you think? Many people were filled with fear, not knowing what it was all about or if there would be another attack. Though you sorrowed for the many that died, the attack and the war that followed are signs that prophesied events are coming to pass. The attacks were a time of great fear for some but also an opportunity of increased faith for others.

Elder Rex D. Pinegar said: "Do not fear the challenges of life, but approach them patiently, with faith in God. He will reward your faith with power not only to endure, but also to overcome hardships, disappointments, trials, and struggles of daily living. Through diligently striving to live the law of God and with faith in Him, we will not be diverted from our eternal course either by the ways or the praise of the world" ("Faith—the Force of Life," *Ensign,* November 1982, 26).

Don't allow fear's grip to overcome you. Remember that you have been promised peace, even in a world filled with fear. The Lord said, "Peace I leave with you, my peace I give unto you: not as the world giveth, give I unto you. Let not your heart be troubled, neither let it be afraid" (John 14:27).

That is a promise from God, and God always keeps his promises.

CHAPTER 11

Great Wickedness

There's something about the topic of this chapter that hits home with most of us. We live in the last days, and we can't go anywhere without seeing or hearing of great wickedness. We turn on the TV and there's wickedness. We open a newspaper and there's wickedness. We go to the mall and there's wickedness. Even a school hallway can be full of wickedness. Widespread wickedness is a fulfillment of prophecy pronounced by the Apostle Paul in the New Testament. He said:

"This know also, that in the *last days* perilous times shall come. For men shall be lovers of their own selves, covetous, boasters, proud, blasphemers, disobedient to parents, unthankful, unholy, without natural affection, trucebreakers, false accusers, incontinent, fierce, despisers of those that are good, traitors, heady, highminded, lovers of pleasures more than lovers of God; having a form of godliness, but denying the power thereof: from such turn away" (2 Timothy 3:1–5; emphasis added).

We're going to take a good look at these verses from Paul because it's important to understand what's happening around us and how we can avoid falling into the pit of wickedness. Remember what can cause fear? Sin. So we must know what to avoid. Let's look at each sin Paul mentions.

1. *Lovers of their own selves.* Such people love the person looking back at them in the mirror more than they love anyone else. You see such people everywhere. They spend lots of time in the bathroom making sure they look just right and lots of time in the mall making sure they dress just right. Life is all about them and what they want. They don't pay any attention to the person sitting next to them who needs help. It would take the focus off of themselves. They're selfish and self-centered and unwilling to sacrifice for others.

2. *Covetous.* Those who covet want something that someone else has. That thing becomes the only thing they think about—even more than God or family. It can be a car, a boat, or a house. But these aren't the things most people covet. Take a look at the following list of coveted items and see if you can relate: someone else's muscles or figure, popularity, parents or family, money, boyfriend or girlfriend, clothing, eyes, musical talent, intelligence, humor, athletic ability, and so forth. The list can be endless. Remember, if you think about it all the time because you want it, it's a sin.

3. *Boasters.* You know who these people are. They believe they have to announce their accomplishments to the world. A quiet, humble acceptance of their achievements is not acceptable to them. They must voice their greatness in order to feel good about themselves. What's ironic is that usually nobody else cares.

4. *Proud.* Those who are proud despise and envy others. We're going to spend an entire chapter on this one later. It's a biggie.

5. *Blasphemers.* Blasphemers are disrespectful toward God and sacred things. Making fun of the Father or the Son, belittling the

sacred, mocking the temple and what Latter-day Saints do there all qualify as blasphemy. Blasphemers are everywhere.

6. *Disobedient to parents.* Being disrespectful to parents means talking back or lying to them, gossiping about them, or refusing to do what they ask. It could also include having a quiet attitude of nastiness toward our parents—rolling our eyes or mumbling under our breath when asked to do something.

7. *Unthankful.* Unthankful people believe the world owes them something—perhaps everything. If something is done for them, it's something they expected. "Why should I thank anyone?" they ask. "I deserve what's been done for me." They need to think again. Many people may serve them, but they commit sin when they refuse to give thanks.

8. *Unholy.* The unholy are not concerned with spiritual things. They make it clear that God is not a priority. The way they dress and the way they act sends a clear message that they have chosen to follow someone else.

9. *Without natural affection.* Natural affection is the love between a man and a woman. "Without natural affection," then, refers to homosexuality. But just because someone struggles with thoughts or feelings toward someone of the same gender doesn't make them sinful. If they resist and redirect those thoughts and feelings, they are doing what God expects of them (Dallin H. Oaks, "Same-Gender Attraction," *Ensign*, October 1995, 8).

10. *Trucebreakers.* Telling an enemy that you're done fighting but then retaliating later is truce breaking. We live in a world of broken promises. It seems that no one keeps promises anymore. As Latter-day Saints, we must be different. God expects us to keep our word.

11. *False accusers.* A false accuser blames others for things they didn't do. Some people do this when they don't want to admit that

they're the one to blame. This can be the biggest cause of fights at school.

12. *Incontinent.* These people have no self-control—no language control, lust control, or thought control. An incontinent person operates according to feelings alone. In other words, "If I feel like it, I'll do it."

13. *Fierce.* Fierce people are angry people. They're angry at their parents, their siblings, their friends, and the world. They pick fights just because they're upset. Even if they have no reason to be angry, they'll find something to make them angry. Again, sin might be at the bottom of this one. People who are doing what's right generally aren't angry.

14. *Despisers of those that are good.* These people are so insecure or guilt-ridden that they mock those who do what's right. If they think you're doing what's right, they'll find a way to make fun of you, such as call you a "Molly Mormon." Can you see how sin can be a powerful motivator for our actions? The miserable love to spread their misery.

15. *Traitors.* In the New Testament this refers to those who are rebellious. They don't listen to their leaders or anyone else in authority. They seek for opportunities to cause problems and feel that their way is always the right way. Whatever the prophet says, they'll do the opposite.

16. *Heady.* Heady people don't make good judgments. They speed down the highway on bullet bikes thinking they're invincible. They live on the edge, seeking one thrill after another, making one rash decision after another. (My grandfather was a mortician. He serviced many people like this.)

17. *Highminded.* This one refers to being stuck-up. If the highminded weren't around, the world would fall apart. Rrrrrright.

18. *Lovers of pleasures more than lovers of God.* This one is all about selfishness. If it feels good in any way, lovers of pleasures want it. This one reminds me of Laman and Lemuel, who repeatedly complained

about having to get the brass plates. But when it was time to fetch the daughters of Ishmael, they didn't whine one bit!

19. *Having a form of godliness, but denying the power thereof.* Among others, these are priesthood holders who don't have faith enough to use the power of God. Or perhaps they're young women who feign righteousness but who aren't committed to the gospel. This one could be called hypocrisy.

"We see our world sinking into depths of corruption," said President Spencer W. Kimball. "Every sin mentioned by Paul is now rampant in our society" ("Voices of the Past, of the Present, of the Future," *Ensign*, June 1971, 17).

I echo the words of Paul: "From such turn away." You can be different. I know you can!

CHAPTER 12

Famine, Pestilence, and Sickness

D o you remember the young woman at the beginning of this book? She was worried about the Second Coming and wondered if there was any hope for her. The things in this chapter freaked her out. But don't skip this chapter just because it sounds scary. These things are important to know. Instead of looking at these signs with fear and terror, remember the purpose of signs:

- They *warn* us and protect us from danger.
- They *motivate* us to prepare for the future.
- They *inspire* us to look forward to the coming of Christ.

What do famine, pestilence, and sickness mean? Famine means food shortage. Pestilence means plague or deadly disease. Sickness means illness, virus, or bad health. Ready or not, here come the prophecies:

- "And there shall be a great hailstorm sent forth to destroy the crops of the earth" (D&C 29:16).

- "And there shall be men standing in that generation, that shall not pass until they shall see an overflowing scourge; for a desolating sickness shall cover the land" (D&C 45:31).
- "Wherefore, I the Lord God will send forth flies upon the face of the earth, which shall take hold of the inhabitants thereof, and shall eat their flesh, and shall cause maggots to come in upon them" (D&C 29:18).

Remember my flies and maggots? Well, the righteous won't go unbothered by the flies, as you will see in a moment, but we can be ready when they show up. Remember that these things will happen to those who don't listen to the Lord. So do what's right—and include a good supply of fly killer with your food storage.

"And there shall be . . . many desolations; *yet men will harden their hearts against me*" (D&C 45:33; emphasis added). You would think people would repent after all this stuff, right? Maybe not.

One of my favorite stories in the Old Testament is the story of Moses and the Pharaoh of Egypt in Exodus 8. Moses was sent by God to persuade Pharaoh to let Israel go. The Israelites had been in bondage to Egypt for more than four hundred years, and now it was time for freedom. But Pharaoh didn't want to let them go. Moses was commanded to send famine, pestilence, and sickness to persuade mighty Pharaoh to give in. It seems at first that this was a battle of wills between Moses and Pharaoh. But there is so much more to the story.

What was God really trying to do with Pharaoh? Could it be possible that God was actually showing him mercy, trying to get him to repent and humble himself? When God's children reach a point that they no longer listen to the still, small voice, God unleashes another tactic to try to humble them (1 Nephi 17:45; D&C 43:20–27). The plagues on Egypt were not-so-subtle reminders that Pharaoh needed to change. Had he done so, he would have been blessed. You know the rest of the story. He never repented, and he ended up destroying most of his army in the Red Sea. It's important to remember that God got his way. He always has. Israel was set free.

Even the great flood in Noah's day was an act of mercy. It prevented his children from sinning even more, and it stopped spirits from being born into the wicked families that then dominated the earth. I hope that you're able to see that often God's ways are not our ways (Isaiah 55:8–9), and he will do whatever is best to save his children.

So why does God send us signs today? Is it because he's angry and enjoys watching his children suffer? Or is it an act of great mercy and compassion—one last attempt to allow his children to repent and come unto him. "Behold, he sendeth an invitation unto all men, for the arms of mercy are extended towards them, and he saith: Repent, and I will receive you" (Alma 5:33).

All right, now that we understand a little more about why God uses famines, pestilence, and sickness, let's figure out how they will affect the righteous. When righteous people live among the wicked, they sometimes experience tribulations resulting from the unrighteousness of their neighbors. The Prophet Joseph Smith said that the "innocent are compelled to suffer for the iniquities of the guilty" (Teachings, 34).

It's not pleasant to hear, but we may suffer along with the wicked even if we're righteous. Remember, this life is a test, and our faith will continue to be tested. However, we have one great benefit to our advantage: living prophets and apostles. They give us counsel and direction on how to prepare for the days that will come.

President Ezra Taft Benson said, "I ask you earnestly, have you provided for your family a year's supply of food, clothing, and, where possible, fuel? The revelation to produce and store food may be as essential to our temporal welfare today as boarding the ark was to the people in the days of Noah" ("To the Fathers in Israel," Ensign, November 1987, 49).

The Lord does love us, and he wants us to be prepared. Could it be that our willingness to follow the counsel of the prophets is an outward demonstration of our desire to obey the Lord? I believe it is.

Elder Bruce R. McConkie told the Saints to prepare so they could be calm when the signs come:

> We do not know when the calamities and troubles of the last days will fall upon any of us as individuals or upon bodies of the Saints. The Lord deliberately withholds from us the day and hour of his coming and of the tribulations which shall precede it—all as part of the testing and probationary experiences of mortality. He simply tells us to watch and be ready.
>
> We can rest assured that if we have done all in our power to prepare for whatever lies ahead, he will then help us with whatever else we need. . . .
>
> We do not say that all of the Saints will be spared and saved from the coming day of desolation. But we do say there is no promise of safety and no promise of security except for those who love the Lord and who are seeking to do all that he commands.
>
> It may be, for instance, that nothing except the power of faith and the authority of the priesthood can save individuals and congregations from the atomic holocausts that surely shall be.
>
> And so we raise the warning voice and say: Take heed; prepare; watch and be ready. There is no security in any course except the course of obedience and conformity and righteousness. ("Stand Independent above All Other Creatures," *Ensign*, May 1979, 93)

I hope you don't feel overwhelmed or that you need to crawl under your bed and hide. Preparing and listening to the prophet will keep us safe. There is no reason for panic if we are ready. President Jedediah M. Grant, a counselor in the First Presidency, said:

"Why is it that the Latter-day Saints are *perfectly calm and serene* among all the convulsions of the earth—the turmoils, strife, war, pestilence, famine and distress of nations? It is because the spirit of prophecy has made known to us that such things would actually transpire upon the earth. We understand it, and view it in its true light. We have learned it by the visions of the Almighty" ("The Hand of God in Events on Earth," *Improvement Era*, February 1915, 286).

A Primary song says it all, "Follow the prophet; he knows the way" (*Children's Songbook*, no. 110).

CHAPTER 13

Extensive Natural Calamities

I remember a show I once saw on tsunamis. Tsunamis are tidal waves that come out of nowhere and can destroy coastal villages and towns. They're caused by earthquakes or volcanic eruptions. On the show I watched, a group of people somewhere in Asia had gathered together on the shore to watch an incoming tsunami. It turned out to be a lot bigger than they thought. They could see it coming from miles away.

The people thought they were protected by the high cement wall they were standing on. But when the big wave came crashing down on them, it swept some of the onlookers off the wall and into the ocean. One man was even swept away with his bicycle. There was nothing anyone could do but watch as about a dozen people were swept out to sea. It made me sick to watch, and I hoped those people were saved.

Tidal waves, floods, earthquakes, hurricanes, and volcanoes are fun to watch on television, but when you're part of a disaster it can be a little more frightening. One of the prophecies of the last days is that the

Lord will preach a sermon called "Natural Calamities" in hopes of persuading his children to repent.

The Lord tells us in the scriptures how he preaches to the world. In the last days, not only will he preach through prophets and apostles but also "by the voice of thunderings, and by the voice of lightnings, and by the voice of tempests, and by the voice of earthquakes, and great hailstorms, and by the voice of famines and pestilences of every kind." The testimony of these natural calamities will come after the testimony of God's servants (D&C 43:25; 88:88–90).

How would you like to be a prophet teaching the importance of repentance while lightening strikes and thunder shakes the earth? It would be awesome. A friend of mine was speaking at church one day during stake seminary graduation. As he was bearing a powerful testimony, an earthquake hit—small but big enough to convince the congregation that the Lord approved of what my friend was saying. On a much larger scale, the Lord will back his prophets with a sermon to welcome the Second Coming. And the world will shake, literally. In fact, it has already begun.

Elder Dallin H. Oaks, commenting on the quaking of the earth in the last days, said:

> These signs of the Second Coming are all around us and seem to be increasing in frequency and intensity. For example, the list of major earthquakes in *The World Almanac and Book of Facts, 2004* shows twice as many earthquakes in the decades of the 1980s and 1990s as in the two preceding decades (189–90). It also shows further sharp increases in the first several years of this century. The list of notable floods and tidal waves and the list of hurricanes, typhoons, and blizzards worldwide show similar increases in recent years (188–89). . . . The accelerating pattern of natural disasters in the last few decades is ominous. ("Preparation for the Second Coming," *Ensign*, May 2004, 7–8)

As we can see, the sermon is underway and the Lord is calling to his children. The time of his coming is near. Remember that the Lord causes calamity so that his rebellious children will repent. If they won't hear the words of a prophet, maybe they'll hear the voice of earthquakes and natural disasters.

Elder Melvin J. Ballard said, "The earthquakes, the sea heaving itself beyond its bounds, bringing such dire destruction as we have seen are the voice of God crying repentance to this generation, a generation that only in part has heeded the warning voice of the servants of the Lord" (in Conference Report, October 1923, 31).

When I was young the biggest calamity I ever experienced was when we ran out of Captain Crunch cereal. But the time has arrived that the Lord is trying to communicate to the world the importance of listening to his words through the prophets. It's time to listen. But if we will not listen to a living prophet who asks us not to get tattoos or unusual body piercings, who discourages immodesty, who warns against immoral and violent movies, and who counsels us not to steady date in high school, who will we listen to? Or maybe we'd better ask, *what* will we listen to? It may be that the only thing that will get some of us to repent will be the power of God that shakes the earth.

The Lord gives us some advice regarding his expectations. He said, "For behold, it is not meet that I should command in all things; for he that is compelled in all things, the same is a slothful and not a wise servant; wherefore he receiveth no reward. Verily I say, men should be anxiously engaged in a good cause, and do many things of their own free will" (D&C 58:26–27).

May we always seek the Lord's will so that when the earth shakes and the calamities come we can take comfort in knowing that we have already made the choice to follow him.

Chapter 14

Signs in the Heavens and the Earth

One of my favorite cartoon shows when I was young (actually, it still is one of my favorites) was *The Jetsons*. It was a show about a family living in the future. They had all kinds of neat gadgets that they used to help out with everyday life, and every episode had to deal with some kind of challenge or adventure. The family even had a dog named Astro, who caused lots of problems for the dad.

One thing that always fascinated me about the show was the way people would drive around in their space cars. They could stop on a dime if they needed to, which they often did because floating out in space were all these traffic signs. Some would turn red or green just like stoplights today; others advertised products.

The signs found in this chapter are similar to the signs in the *The Jetsons*. They don't sit out in space and tell us whether to stop or go, but they give us information that will keep us safe as we travel toward the Second Coming. Remember that one of the purposes of signs is to show us that Christ's coming is near and that we should be looking forward to it. So let's start with the signs in heaven. What kind of signs are we talking about?

Think for a moment about the days of the prophet Joshua. He was the prophet after Moses was taken into heaven. Joshua did some incredible things. He conquered Jericho and did all kinds of cool stuff. One of the coolest was when he commanded the sun and the moon to stand still (Joshua 10:12–14). That's the kind of sign we're talking about—the universe around us doing interesting and unusual things.

"The episode of Joshua commanding the sun and moon to stand still was insignificant compared to the stellar upsets that will accompany the second advent of the Savior, when stars will be hurled from their places," Elder Mark E. Peterson wrote. "Some power will darken the sun and make the moon refuse to give its light" (*Joshua: Man of Faith*, 58–59).

God is so powerful that he can cause many great things to happen. If he wants to hold the earth still, he can do so. If he wants to turn the moon blood red or stop the sun from shining on the earth, he can do that too. He can even cause stars to fall from their places. It's all a wonderful display of his cosmic power, for he is the creator of the universe.

The scriptures tell us that before Christ comes we will see such wonders in the heavens and on the earth. We will behold "blood, and fire, and vapors of smoke." The sun "shall be darkened," the moon will "be turned into blood," and the stars will "fall from heaven" (D&C 45:41–42).

Here are some other interesting thoughts about the signs in the heavens. President Joseph Fielding Smith said:

> One wonders if we are not now seeing some of the signs in heaven—not all, for undoubtedly some of them will be among the heavenly bodies, such as the moon and the sun, the meteors and comets, but in speaking of the heavens, reference is made to that part which surrounds the earth and which belongs to it. It is in the

atmosphere where many of the signs are to be given. Do we not see airships of various kinds traveling through the heavens daily? Have we not had signs in the earth and through the earth with the radio, railroad trains, automobiles, submarines, and satellites, and in many other ways? There are yet to be great signs: the heavens are to be shaken, the sign of the Son of Man is to be given, and then shall the tribes of the earth mourn." (In Conference Report, April 1966, 13, 15)

To you and me some of these things, such as airplanes, seem commonplace. But they are signs that we are getting closer to the coming of Christ. No other age in the history of the world has had what we have, and we should see technological wonders as signs and as prophecies being fulfilled.

What about signs in the earth? Whenever I think of these kinds of signs, I see other miracles that we view as normal things. Cars, televisions, computers, and all kinds of other ordinary things are miracles. All of these signs are proof that the Second Coming is closer than we think.

One of the greatest resources we have regarding signs on the earth is found in the Book of Mormon. Shortly before Jesus visited the Nephites, many things occurred that are a type of the events that will happen before he returns. These include thunderings and lightnings. The Book of Mormon says the thunder was so loud that it seemed as if the earth was going to crack in half. Cool! In fact the earth did tremble and shake, and the land was broken up. After the destruction had ended, the people didn't even recognize much of the land because it had changed so much.

The storms and the tornadoes, or what the Book of Mormon calls "whirlwinds," were incredible. The people had never seen or heard of anything like them before. Mountains were laid low, valleys were raised, and cities were sunk. It was the ultimate thrill ride! Highways were broken up, and there was no way to get around. That would be interesting to experience today! We might just find out how interesting.

"For not many days hence and the earth shall tremble and reel to and fro as a drunken man; and the sun shall hide his face, and shall refuse to give light; and the moon shall be bathed in blood; and the stars shall become exceedingly angry, and shall cast themselves down as a fig that falleth from off a fig-tree" (D&C 88:87).

The Lord's presence will be so great that "the sun shall hide his face in shame, and the moon shall withhold its light, and the stars shall be hurled from their places" (D&C 133:49).

Concerning these prophecies, President Wilford Woodruff said: "These things are about to come to pass upon the heads of the present generation, notwithstanding they are not looking for it, neither do they believe it. Yet their unbelief will not make the truth of God of none effect. The signs are appearing in the heavens and on the earth, and all things indicate the fulfillment of the Prophets. . . . Why should not God reveal His secrets unto His servants the Prophets, that the Saints might be led in paths of safety, and escape those evils which are about to engulf a whole generation in ruin?" (History of the Church, 6:27).

President Gordon B. Hinckley has added that the vision of Joel is being fulfilled in which he declared, "And I will shew wonders in the heavens and in the earth, blood, and fire, and pillars of smoke. The sun shall be turned into darkness, and the moon into blood, before the great and the terrible day of the Lord come" ("Living in the Fulness of Times," Ensign, November 2001, 4; Joel 2:30–31).

May we look for the signs all around us that testify that Christ lives and that his coming is near.

CHAPTER 15

The Gospel Preached to Every Nation

One of the greatest moments in a young person's life is the day a mission call arrives. Family members gather around as the prospective missionary prepares to open the letter from Church headquarters. With trembling hands, the elder or sister quickly opens the letter and reads the call. "Japan," "Australia," or "Boise" might be the place they read out loud. When I read "Philippines," some members of my family thought I said "Philadelphia." I had to read it again. Then they all went quiet. We discovered that the Philippines were a lot farther away than Philadelphia.

The Lord expects every worthy male to serve a mission. He said, "And this gospel shall be preached unto every nation, and kindred, and tongue, and people. And the servants of God shall go forth, saying with a loud voice: Fear God and give glory to him, for the hour of his judgment is come" (D&C 133:37–38).

Why does the Lord place so much importance on missionary work? He tells us, "And that every man should take righteousness in his hands and faithfulness upon his loins, and lift a warning voice unto the inhabitants of the earth; and declare both by word and by flight that desolation shall come upon the wicked" (D&C 63:37).

Did you note that he said "every man"? By that he also meant every boy who is becoming a man. President Gordon B. Hinckley clarified that point when he said, "Missionary work is essentially a priesthood responsibility. As such, our young men must carry the major burden. This is their responsibility and their obligation" ("Some Thoughts on Temples, Retention of Converts, and Missionary Service," *Ensign*, November 1997, 52).

Two decades earlier President Spencer W. Kimball declared, "Should every young man fill a mission? And the answer of the Church is yes, and the answer of the Lord is yes. Enlarging this answer we say: Certainly every male member of the Church *should* fill a mission" ("Planning for a Full and Abundant Life," *Ensign*, May 1974, 87).

The Lord wants every worthy male to serve a mission because that is the way the gospel can reach people all over the world. We could make a big megaphone and shout our message to the world from Salt Lake City, but what would that accomplish? We already do that with general conference. Church broadcasts reach around the globe, but broadcasts don't replace missionaries. The Lord not only wants people to hear the gospel but also to grow in the gospel.

The Lord gave us the reason that missionary work is so important. He said: "Behold, vengeance cometh speedily upon the inhabitants of the earth, a day of wrath, a day of burning, a day of desolation, of weeping, of mourning, and of lamentation; and as a whirlwind it shall come upon all the face of the earth, saith the Lord. . . . But purify your hearts before me; and then go ye into all the world, and preach my gospel unto every creature who has not received it; and he that believeth and is baptized shall be saved, and he that believeth not, and is not baptized, shall be damned" (D&C 112:24, 28–29).

We must proclaim the gospel so that the world will have the opportunity to be saved when Christ comes. Many people are waiting for the gospel to be preached to them. But gospel preaching alone will not save them. They must be baptized and confirmed members of the Church. They must receive the priesthood and go to the temple to receive their endowment. They must be married in the temple for time and all eternity. They must serve their fellow Saints and endure to the end. All of this cannot happen unless missionaries go to every nation and live among the people they serve.

God expects his covenant people to warn his children of the Second Coming and help them prepare for it. Those young men who do not serve missions—leaving their duties undone and ignoring their priesthood responsibilities—may actually be breaking a covenant (D&C 84:33–41).

President Kimball said, "Declining to serve when called may constitute a sin of omission as well as one of commission. Certainly it is a sin of omission to accept responsibility, to covenant with the Lord, and then fail to do the work as well as possible. . . . One breaks the priesthood covenant by transgressing commandments—but also by leaving undone his duties. Accordingly, to break this covenant one needs only to do nothing" (The Miracle of Forgiveness, 95–96).

President John Taylor said, "If you do not magnify your callings, God will hold you responsible for those whom you might have saved had you done your duty" (in Journal of Discourses, 20:23–24). God loves his children, and it's up to us to help bring them to Christ.

So what about those nations whose doors are closed to missionary work? Before the Lord comes in his glory, you will see those doors open. Even now the Lord is causing great miracles to take place that will open those doors. Hearts are being softened and missionaries are needed to fill the world. Look at this wonderful example by Elder Earl C. Tingey of how miracles are taking place today to allow the gospel to be preached to all the world:

A dozen years ago, in one of the countries of Africa, we had faithful members of the Church who had been meeting in their homes for several years. I went to that country to see if we could receive permission from the government to bring in missionaries and establish the Church. I met with a high-ranking government minister. He gave me 20 minutes to explain our position.

When I finished, he said, "I do not see where anything you have told me is any different from what is currently available in our country. I see no reason to approve your request to bring missionaries into our country."

He stood up to usher me out of his office. I was panic-stricken. I had failed. In a moment our meeting would be over. What could I do? I offered a silent prayer.

Then I had an inspired thought. I said to the minister, "Sir, if you will give me five more minutes, I would like to share one other thought with you. Then I will leave." He kindly consented.

I reached for my wallet and removed this small *For the Strength of Youth* booklet, which I have always carried.

I said, "This is a little booklet of standards we give all of the youth in our Church."

I then read some of the standards. . . . When I finished, he said, "You mean to tell me you expect the youth of your church to live these standards?"

"Yes," I replied, "and they do."

"That is amazing," he said. "Could you send me some of these booklets so that I could distribute them to the youth of my church?"

I replied, "Yes," and I did.

Several months later we received official approval from the government of that country to come and establish the Church. ("For the Strength of Youth," *Ensign*, May 2004, 50)

The Lord's work will march on. Faithful missionaries will serve. Thousands will join the Church because of their efforts. And miracles will be performed as nations allow the Lord's Church to blossom on their soil. It will happen. It is happening.

Don't allow yourself to watch from a distance. Be a part of the army whose general is the Lord himself. Serve a mission. The Lord needs you, and you need the experience, wisdom, faith, and endurance that come from serving a mission. Because of the growth that comes from serving the Lord selflessly for two years, a mission can prepare you for the Second Coming like no other experience can.

CHAPTER 16

Gathering of the Righteous and the Wicked

P *arables*. What in the world are parables? The word sounds like "pair of bulls," but that's not what they are. To understand this chapter and what the Savior wants us to know, we have to start with the meaning of parables. "Parables are short stories which point up and illustrate spiritual truths" (McConkie, *Doctrinal New Testament Commentary*, 1:283). In other words, parables are stories that teach us something we need to know to improve our lives or to prepare for the second coming of the Savior.

We're going to take a look at an interesting parable that the Savior taught about the gathering of the righteous and the wicked and why that gathering needs to take place before the Second Coming. In the parable a man plants good seeds in his fields. But something terrible happens. While he's sleeping an enemy plants something called "tares" among his wheat. What's so bad about tares? Tares are weeds that look a lot like wheat. They have a bitter taste, and if eaten alone or accidentally mixed with wheat for bread, they can cause dizziness and violent vomiting (Matthew 13:24–29; McConkie, *Doctrinal New Testament Commentary,* 1:296).

So how could the man rid his field of the tares? If he tried pulling up the tares while the plants were young, he might end up pulling the good wheat along with the bad tares. That would be tragic. Some of us do that when we're weeding. We accidentally pull up flowers or a vegetable plant because when they're young they often look the same as a weed.

What do you think the owner of the field did? He said, "Let both grow together until the harvest: and in the time of harvest I will say to the reapers, Gather ye together first the tares, and bind them in bundles to burn them: but gather the wheat into my barn" (Matthew 13:30).

What a wise man! He allowed the tares and the wheat to grow together, and then the reapers gathered them separately for either burning or storing. The field represents the world, the wheat represents the righteous, and the tares represent the wicked. Can you see how the same thing is happening today? Even in school you can see a gathering take place. There are drama people, band members, athletes, chess club members, and so on. It doesn't really matter which group or club you belong to. What matters is, are those groups wheat or tares? Generally speaking, good people don't hang out with the rough crowd and vice versa.

The Lord makes another interesting point found in the Doctrine and Covenants: "Behold, verily I say unto you, the angels are crying unto the Lord day and night, who are ready and waiting to be sent forth to reap down the fields" (86:5). That verse makes it seem as if the wheat and the tares are now grown and it's harvest time. In other words, it's time for the angels to come and do what they have been waiting to do—separate the righteous from the wicked so that the righteous will be spared and the wicked will be burned.

The Prophet Joseph Smith recorded that revelation in 1832. I wonder how much closer we are to the harvest now? And what's going on with those impatient angels, whose job it is to reap? President Joseph Fielding Smith was present when President Wilford Woodruff talked about these angels at the dedication of the Salt Lake Temple (*Signs of the Times*, 112–13).

President Smith recorded that the time of the harvest had arrived:

> The Lord said that the sending forth of these angels was to be at the end of the harvest, and the harvest is the end of the world. Now, that ought to cause us some very serious reflections. And the angels have been pleading, as I have read it to you, before the Lord to be sent on their mission. Until 1893 the Lord said to them no, *and then He set them loose.* According to the revelation of President Woodruff, the *Lord sent them out on that mission.* What do we gather out of that? That we are at the time of the end. This is the time of the harvest. This is the time spoken of which is called the end of the world. (*Signs of the Times*, 121; emphasis added)

The time has come. The gathering is taking place. You can see this all around the world—people siding with either Satan or Christ. Some people are living the gospel and defending it with their testimonies and lives; others don't care and are more interested in following the crowd.

Now is the time to take a stand and choose Christ. You can do it. Maybe you are struggling with certain challenges in your life. Maybe sin has overcome you. Know that you can change. That's the great blessing of the Atonement. Make a decision now to be a better person. Start hanging out with the kids at school who are striving to do what's right. You may not become popular because of that choice, but doing what's right is not about popularity; it's about following the Lord.

Several years ago a young man was asked to sing a solo in a high school assembly. He was somewhat shy but agreed to sing. The day came, and he summoned up all the courage he had and stepped out on the stage. The auditorium was filled to capacity. All of his friends and peers were watching. The music started and he began to sing. About halfway through his song, someone in the back of the auditorium peeled an orange and threw it at him. It hit the boy in the stomach, and he gasped for air. Many in the audience laughed, but many more were upset. With tears in his eyes, the boy finished his song, and with orange all over him made his way off the stage.

At that moment another young man unexpectedly ran to the stage. He was the kind of guy that most people made fun of. He didn't have many friends, and he spent most of his time alone at school, hugging the walls of the hallway as he made his way around. But this day he was different. He stepped on the stage and grabbed the microphone. He began to compliment the boy for singing. Then he told the person who threw the orange how disappointed he was and how he demanded an apology. The entire school clapped and cheered for him. I still remember his name: Rand.

I was the boy who sang the song. Dripping with orange and humiliated, I learned that day what taking a stand meant. It means that even in the most difficult moments of life we are willing to defend our beliefs and other people. I will never forget that experience. I will never forget Rand. That day he became a hero.

May we, like Rand, take the side of Christ in preparation for the harvest. May we be found with the rest of the wheat, gathered together, as we look forward to that incredible day.

CHAPTER 17

"The Lamanites Shall Blossom As the Rose"

Whenever we hear the word *Lamanite*, most of us think of Laman and Lemuel, the sons of Lehi. Or we may think of the great battles in the Book of Mormon that took place between the Lamanites and the Nephites. We even reflect on the wicked Lamanite king Amalickiah, who swore with an oath that he would drink the blood of Captain Moroni. (Amalickiah was actually a Nephite by birth.) We may even envision the final great battle between the Nephites and the Lamanites, when hundreds of thousands of Nephites were killed. The Lamanites seemed to be a curse to the Nephites, who, for most of Book of Mormon history, wanted to live in peace. It's easy to get caught up in negative stories about the Lamanites, but the Lord has special blessings in store for their descendants.

If you think carefully about it, the Lamanites actually had a history similar to that of the Nephites. They had times of wickedness and times of righteousness. For a while the Lamanites were even more righteous than the Nephites. They even had great prophets, just like the Nephites. Here are some of their positive traits:

- They were good at keeping oaths (Alma 44:15).
- They could be compassionate (Mosiah 19:13–14).
- They generally treated women well (Jacob 2:34–35).
- When converted, they became extraordinarily faithful and industrious (Alma 23:6–7, 18; 24:6, 18).

Granted, the Lamanites were predominantly wicked, but God always had something in mind for them. He knew that at a future day the Lamanites would be ready to hear the gospel, and when they did they would be incredibly faithful.

The Lord said, "Before the great day of the Lord shall come, Jacob shall flourish in the wilderness, and the *Lamanites shall blossom as the rose.* Zion shall flourish upon the hills and rejoice upon the mountains, and shall be assembled together unto the place which I have appointed" (D&C 49:24–25; emphasis added).

God loves all of his children and wants them to come to the gospel. He welcomes all with open arms (Alma 5:33). The Lamanites of today have a special promise—that they will blossom as a rose and become a powerhouse in the Church. Even now that prophecy is being fulfilled. Thousands of people in South America and Central America are joining the Church. Not only are they joining, but they are also leading. This is a fulfillment of the Lord's words about the descendents of Lehi. They have blossomed and will continue to be a strength in the Church.

Elder Jeffrey R. Holland, describing the faithfulness of these great people, said:

> I wish you could meet the sister called to serve with us from her native Argentina. Wanting to do everything possible to finance her own mission, she sold her violin, her most prized and nearly sole earthly possession. She said simply, "God will bless me

with another violin after I have blessed His children with the gospel of Jesus Christ."

I wish you could meet the Chilean elder who, living without family in a boarding school, happened upon a Book of Mormon and started reading it that very evening. . . . He read insatiably—nonstop through the night. With the breaking of day, he was overwhelmed with a profound sense of peace and a new spirit of hope. He determined to find out where this book had come from and who had written its marvelous pages. Thirteen months later he was on a mission.

I wish you could meet the marvelous young man who came to us from Bolivia, arriving with no matching clothing and shoes three sizes too large for him. He was a little older because he was the sole breadwinner in his home, and it had taken some time to earn money for his mission. He raised chickens and sold the eggs door-to-door. Then, just as his call finally came, his widowed mother faced an emergency appendectomy. Our young friend gave every cent of the money he had earned for his mission to pay for his mother's surgery and postoperative care, then quietly rounded up what used clothing he could from friends and arrived at the MTC in Santiago on schedule. I can assure you that his clothes now match, his shoes now fit, and both he and his mother are safe and sound, temporally as well as spiritually. ("Abide in Me," *Ensign*, May 2004, 30)

The Lamanites of today are a chosen generation. And just like many of their righteous ancestors, they are faithful and ready to serve as leaders in the Church during the Millennium. It's awesome to live in a day in which the Lord is fulfilling his promises to them.

CHAPTER 18

False Christs and False Prophets

There shall also arise false Christs, and false prophets, and shall show great signs and wonders, insomuch, that, if possible, they shall deceive the very elect" (JS–M 1:22).

That's a frightening thought! In the last days, false Christs and false prophets may deceive the "very elect." The "elect" refers to those who have heard the Savior's voice, accepted his gospel, and received the priesthood (D&C 29:7; 84:33–34). What can we do to prevent ourselves from being deceived by these imposters? This chapter will answer that question, help us identify the imposters, and show us the tactics they will use.

First of all, I would like to make an announcement. God has chosen fifteen incredible men to lead this Church as he wants it led. If we follow them, we will not be deceived. Well, that was easy. Just keep your eyes and ears focused on the Lord's true prophets and apostles, and you will never go astray.

"Yes, we believe in a living prophet, seer, and revelator, and I bear you my solemn witness that we have a living prophet, seer, and revelator," testified President Harold B. Lee. He added, "God will never permit him to lead us astray. As has been said, God would remove us out of our place if we should attempt to do it. You have no concern" ("The Place of the Living Prophet, Seer, and Revelator," 13).

So what's the big deal about false Christs and prophets? Apparently the Lord himself is concerned because he states that many will follow after them. Let's do some investigating and discover what a false Christ or prophet is. That will give us a better idea of what to look for if we ever see one.

Do you remember the story of Korihor in the Book of Mormon? He showed up in the capital city of Zarahemla one day and started teaching crazy things. The philosophies he taught are the same teachings that false prophets use today.

First, he taught that there would be no Christ and no prophecies, stating that such beliefs were foolishness (Alma 30:12–14). Trying to destroy an individual's testimony of the redeemer of the world is what false prophets do.

Next, he taught that we can't know of things to come (Alma 30:13). He tried to destroy the people's belief in the true prophets, claiming that their prophecies were false. A sign of false prophets is that they will attack the teachings of a real prophet. Then they will teach that we can't believe in what we can't see (Alma 30:15). False prophets go to the heart of our religion, which is individual faith. If you remember, faith is belief in something we can't see (Alma 32:21). A false prophet tries to destroy our faith in God by promoting himself. It's as if he wants to take the place of God.

Korihor also taught that there is no sin and no forgiveness (Alma 30:16). Isn't that great? If people believe there is no sin and no forgiveness, guess what they give themselves permission to do? Anything! "Eat, drink, and be merry, for tomorrow we die" (2 Nephi

28:7). In other words, a false prophet tries to get us to believe that there is no crime in sin and no responsibility associated with bad choices.

Korihor's last teaching was that there is no afterlife. He said that when we die, it's all over. There's nothing else (Alma 30:18).

Elder M. Russell Ballard warned about false prophets and false teachers:

> Therefore, let us beware of false prophets and false teachers, both men and women, who are self-appointed declarers of the doctrines of the Church and who seek to spread their false gospel and attract followers by sponsoring symposia, books, and journals *whose contents challenge fundamental doctrines of the Church. Beware of those who speak and publish in opposition to God's true prophets and who actively proselyte others with reckless disregard for the eternal well-being of those whom they seduce.* Like Nehor and Korihor in the Book of Mormon, they rely on sophistry to deceive and entice others to their views. They "set themselves up for a light unto the world, that they may get gain and praise of the world; but they seek not the welfare of Zion" (2 Nephi 26:29). ("Beware of False Prophets and False Teachers," *Ensign*, November 1999, 63; emphasis added)

The scary thing about Korihor is that he had great success. Many people in the Book of Mormon were deceived by Korihor because they took their focus off the prophet—Alma—and started to believe in false teachings "because they were pleasing unto the carnal mind" (Alma 30:53). In other words, sin without consequence sounds good to the natural man. But it's a big lie.

You may be thinking, "That's great, but I will never be stupid enough to follow a guy like Korihor. His teachings go totally against what I believe." Let's examine that for just a minute. Maybe a guy like Korihor doesn't march into your town and start saying all this stuff, but his teachings have crept into books, television shows, movies, classrooms, courthouses, and governments, and some of us believe them. Below are some thoughts we may have that reflect Korihor's false teachings.

Some of us may think, *The scriptures aren't that important. I don't have to read them every day.* Korihor said, "These things which ye call prophecies . . . are foolish traditions" (Alma 30:14).

Some of us may think, *Praying is not that important; no one hears me anyway.* Korihor said, "Ye cannot know of things which ye do not see" (Alma 30:15)

Some of us may think, *I'll sin today and repent later; it's no big deal.* Korihor said, "Whatsoever a man [does is] no crime" (Alma 30:17).

We can be also influenced by the teachings of the ultimate false prophet, Satan. We must fight his teachings every day because even the very elect are being deceived by him. But we can overcome him if we listen to the Spirit and do not give in to temptation.

Elder Bruce R. McConkie wrote: "A false Christ is not a person. It is a false system of worship, a false church, a false cult that says: 'Lo, here is salvation; here is the doctrine of Christ. Come and believe thus and so, and ye shall be saved.' *It is any concept or philosophy that says that redemption, salvation, sanctification, justification, and all of the promised rewards can be gained in any way except that set forth by the apostles and prophets*" (*The Millennial Messiah*, 48; emphasis added).

Let's join together to fight the Korihor thoughts of this world. You *can* have greater faith in Christ. You *can* have great trust in his prophets and apostles. Look to the scriptures for spiritual nourishment, and pray that God's spirit will always guide you to know the way. He *will* answer your prayers, and he *will* give you strength to overcome the Korihors of life.

PART THREE

WHAT WILL HAPPEN WHEN HE COMES?

CHAPTER 19

What Will Happen to the Earth?

One of our favorite places to go for family vacation is called Craters of the Moon in Idaho. It's a weird place that's covered with miles and miles of black lava rocks and dormant volcanoes. It looks much like the surface of the moon, except that there's no vegetation on the moon. Craters, at least, has a few trees and some sagebrush. Nearby, there's a place called Hell's Half Acre. The name says it all. It's similar to Craters of the Moon, but it's more burned looking.

Whenever I have an opportunity to look across the area's bleak nothingness, I imagine what the earth will look like after Jesus comes. I wonder if it will end up being a barren world of black nothingness, with mist rising from the depths of the cracks in the rocks. Sounds pretty unpleasant, but what's really going to happen to the earth? Well, there are actually three major things that will happen when Christ comes.

First, the scriptures tell us the earth will be burned to a crisp when he comes again (Jacob 6:3). Christ himself will burn the earth. Christ is a celestial being. We often compare the glory of celestial beings to the sun. It's hot already in the middle of July, but imagine if the sun got any closer to the earth. It wouldn't be long before the earth would be in flames. Christ has that kind of glory (D&C 76:70). His presence will be so radiant that the earth's inhabitants will be "consumed away and utterly destroyed by the brightness of [his] coming" (D&C 5:19; McConkie, *Doctrinal New Testament Commentary*, 3:368–69). Another thing that will happen to the earth is that all the land masses will come together into one. Remember the massive earthquakes mentioned earlier? When Christ stands on the Mount of Olives, there will be an earthquake the likes of which the world has never known. The oceans will gather into one place, and the land will become one. It'll be cool! You'll be able to drive to Japan, England, or Hawaii. All countries and continents will come together and be united in preparation for the Lord to be their king.

"He shall command the great deep, and it shall be driven back into the north countries, and the islands shall become one land; and the land of Jerusalem and the land of Zion shall be turned back into their own place, and the earth shall be like as it was in the days before it was divided" (D&C 133:23–24).

Joseph Fielding Smith said, "By looking at a wall map of the world, you will discover how the land surface along the northern and southern coast of the American Hemisphere and Europe and Africa has the appearance of having been together at one time. Of course, there have been many changes on the earth's surface since the beginning. We are informed by revelation that the time will come when this condition will be changed and that the land surface of the earth will come back again as it was in the beginning and all be in one place" (*Answers to Gospel Questions*, 5:73–74).

But what good is having the land masses come together if they're nothing but a massive charred chunk of land that looks like Craters of the Moon or Hell's Half Acre? Doesn't seem very pleasant, does it? Thankfully, we have Church doctrine to help us understand the third thing that will happen when Christ comes. The tenth article of faith says the earth will be renewed and receive its paradisiacal glory. The word *paradisiacal* contains the word *paradise*. That sounds a lot better than Hell's Half Acre!

"This earth was created in a new or paradisiacal state; then, incident to Adam's transgression, it fell to its present telestial state," Elder Bruce R. McConkie wrote. "At the Second Coming of our Lord, it will be *renewed, regenerated, refreshed, transfigured*, become again *a new earth, a paradisiacal earth*. Its millennial status will be a return to its pristine state of beauty and glory, the state that existed before the fall" (*Mormon Doctrine*, 796; emphasis added).

Can you imagine living in a place like the Garden of Eden? Wow! I can hardly wait to experience that new world when Christ comes. That's something to look forward to and be excited about. But there's more. The deserts and dry places of the earth will be changed into beautiful gardens. Pools of water will give life to the land. "And in the barren deserts there shall come forth pools of living water; and the parched ground shall no longer be a thirsty land" (D&C 133:29).

It's even possible that the axis of the earth will be altered so that the change in seasons ceases, enabling us to grow fruits and vegetables year-round (McConkie, *A New Witness for the Articles of Faith*, 649–50). It will be a new world for us to live in—a place of peace and safety, a place where God can bless his righteous children.

So get rid of any ideas about some nasty looking piece of charcoal for an earth. We have so much to look forward to if we are righteous. God's greatest blessings are being saved for the faithful, one of them being an incredible new world.

CHAPTER 20

What Will Happen to the Wicked?

When I was about eight years old, some friends and I were playing in a big field behind the apartment complex where we lived. We were having a great time just being with each other and acting a little crazy. After a while I noticed out of the corner of my eye that someone was approaching us from the other end of the field. He was a new kid to the neighborhood, and as he slowly walked toward us, he asked if he could join us. A horrible thought crossed my mind: *See if you can hit him with a rock.* I really liked the group I was in, and the thought of someone else playing with us, especially someone I didn't know, really bothered me. The rock idea sounded good.

I challenged my friends to see if they could hit him. As each one tried, I watched the new boy back farther and farther away from us. I got irritated with my friends and picked up a rock the size of my fist. Because they couldn't hit him, I would. I threw the rock as hard as I could, letting it fly through the air like a professional baseball pitcher.

The next thing I knew the new kid was lying on the ground. The rock had hit him square in the forehead and knocked him out! My friends quickly decided that it was time to go home. I stood alone, looking at the boy from a distance. I could see he was hurt. The rock had cut a big gash in his head. My gut instinct told me to go help him, to run to his side, and carry him home, where his parents could get him to the hospital. Instead, I ran home.

When I got home I went up to my bedroom and hid under the bed, hoping I wouldn't get in trouble. So much for hope. Moments later a knock came at the door; it was the new kid's dad. My mom knew where I was (moms always know where you are) and called me downstairs, where I was required to tell what happened. I was horrified. The kid's dad was about 6-foot-5. But he handled the situation well. Apparently his son had come to his senses and stumbled home. His parents then took him to the emergency room, where he received several stitches. I felt terrible about what I had done. You probably feel terrible about what I did too.

The happy side to this story is that the boy recovered, and we actually became best friends. But at the time, I thought I was the worst kid in the world. I wanted to hide, which is exactly how the wicked will feel when Christ comes again. The prophet Alma said: "For our words will condemn us, yea, all our works will condemn us; we shall not be found spotless; and our thoughts will also condemn us; and in this awful state we shall not dare to look up to our God; and we would fain be glad if we could command the rocks and the mountains to fall upon us to hide us from his presence" (Alma 12:14).

Have you ever done something wrong and wished you could hide? I still remember how mean I was to that new boy, but I feel much better about that experience today, knowing that I have long since repented of my wickedness. So what will happen to the wicked when Christ comes? Malachi tells us they'll be burned (Malachi 4:1). Let's do a study of wickedness and find out just who the wicked are that will be destroyed at the Second Coming.

The apostle Paul tells us that all people are not the same. There are actually three kinds of people: celestial, terrestrial, and telestial (1 Corinthians 15:40–41). Which one of these three groups is considered wicked? Celestial? No, celestial people repent, apply the Atonement in their lives, and develop valiant testimonies (D&C 76:50–70). How about terrestrial people? Well, these are honorable people who have been deceived by Satan. They have chosen not to follow Christ while on the earth (D&C 76:71–80).

That brings us to the last group of people: the telestials. The scriptures describe telestial people as liars, adulterers, murderers, and those who reject the prophets and the gospel (D&C 76:98–106). Of these three groups, then, which ones are wicked?

President Joseph Fielding Smith said, "When the reign of Jesus Christ comes during the millennium, *only those who have lived the telestial law will be removed.* The earth will be cleansed of all its corruption and wickedness. Those who have lived virtuous lives, who have been honest in their dealings with their fellow man and have endeavored to do good to the best of their understanding, shall remain. . . . The honest and upright of all nations, kindreds, and beliefs, who have kept the *terrestrial or celestial law,* will remain" (*Doctrines of Salvation,* 3:62–63; emphasis added).

There you have it! Those who live celestial and terrestrial lives will be spared while those who live telestial lives will be destroyed. What does that mean for you? Should you be saying to yourself, "I don't have to try so hard because I can be a terrestrial person and be just fine." No! God will give his greatest blessings only to those who live celestial lives. He wants all of us to be celestial. That's the only way we will be able to live with him again. Those who are terrestrial or telestial will not return to the presence of our Father in Heaven (D&C 76:77, 86).

The moral of this chapter is this: Don't throw rocks at people. And if you do, use the Atonement in your life, repent, and strengthen your testimony of Christ every day. Then you will be prepared both for celestial glory and for Christ when he comes in his glory. You will experience what we're going to talk about in the next chapter. So keep reading.

CHAPTER 21

What Will Happen to the Righteous?

Have you ever accomplished something that was important to you? Maybe you passed a test or made a new friend. Maybe you set a personal record in a sporting event or played a solo well in a recital. Whatever your personal success was, I'm sure it was a great experience for you. Let me tell you a story about a person I know who succeeded.

Toward the beginning of every year, high schools and colleges across the country have a major competition. Some say these contests are bigger than any sporting event or any final exam. Many students spend months, if not years, preparing for them. What are they? Annual bridge-building contests, of course. Yes, students from all over the country compete to see if they can build a small bridge that will withstand the heaviest weight.

One particular year a student put all of his efforts into his bridge. He studied, planned, glued, and pasted until he had completed his project. The day of the competition came, and he took his bridge to be tested. One hundred pounds, then two hundred pounds, then three hundred pounds were placed on his bridge. The weight kept going up and up. Everyone was excited but not as excited as the bridge builder. Finally, at around a thousand pounds, his bridge broke.

The competition lasted the rest of the day, with other students bringing their bridges to be tested. At the end of the day, during an assembly, the winning bridge builder was announced. To his surprise the student who had studied and worked so hard heard his name called.

I looked at him and could tell he couldn't believe it! He could hardly get out of his seat when he was called to the front of the auditorium. Finally, he made his way to the stage and was awarded his trophy in front of the entire school. He was cheered by his peers and congratulated by his friends as he returned to his seat. It was a day of triumph. He had worked so hard to become the master bridge builder.

This is obviously an example of how good it can feel to succeed when you've worked hard at something. Striving every day to be good is like building a bridge. It takes time, patience, and energy. You have to know the plan—the plan of salvation—and how it works. You have to apply the glue of obedience and prayer. Then, when the test comes, you'll be able to withstand the pressure of temptation. What happens if you're doing your best when Christ comes? What's your reward? Rest assured that it will be much greater than any earthly trophy.

Just before Christ burns the earth with his glory and destroys the wicked by fire, he will save the righteous. "And the saints (meaning the righteous) that are upon the earth, who are alive, shall be quickened and be caught up to meet him" (D&C 88:96).

In other words, if we're righteous we'll be called to the front of the auditorium to receive our reward, and our reward will be to enjoy the presence of the Savior. What a great thing to think about! I don't know exactly how we'll "be caught up to meet him," but it's exciting to imagine being part of a group of righteous people rising heavenward and approaching the Savior. Something will happen to us during that journey. A change will take place in us so we can enjoy Christ's presence and not be consumed.

Then, after the earth is burned, we'll return. Remember, by then the earth will be one land mass and will have become like the Garden of Eden. We will return to enjoy the reward of our righteous living. We will have children, enjoy our families, listen to the Savior and his prophets, and go on with our lives—all in the absence of wickedness and temptation. Sounds great, doesn't it! Then, after we reach the age of one hundred years, we will die (Isaiah 65:20). But even death will be different. We will not be buried when we *die* because we'll be changed in the twinkling of an *eye*. (Hey, that rhymed). We'll be twinkled! (D&C 63:51).

Remember the promises mentioned in chapter two? Life on the paradisiacal earth will be when all of those promises are fulfilled for the righteous. Elder Boyd K. Packer made a great statement about being good. He said:

> I will not consent to any influence from the adversary. I have come to know what power he has. I know all about that. But I also have come to know the power of truth and of righteousness and of good, and I want to be good. I'm not ashamed to say that—I want to be good. And I've found in my life that it has been critically important that this was established between me and the Lord so that I knew that he knew which way I committed my agency. I went before him and said, "I'm not neutral, and you can do with me what you want. If you need my vote, it's there. I don't care what you do with me, and you don't have to take anything from me because I give it to you—everything, all I own, all I am—," and that makes the difference. ("To Those Who Teach in Troubled Times," 76)

As you go about building the righteous bridges of your life, remember the great day to come. You will be called up to meet the Savior, and you will be filled with joy as you realize that your efforts to read the scriptures, pray, keep the commandments, magnify your Church callings, love your family and your neighbor, and serve the Lord will be rewarded. He will come and bring with him all the peace that has been prepared for those who love him.

He has said: "Verily, verily, I say unto you, ye are little children, and ye have not as yet understood how great blessings the Father hath in his own hands and prepared for you; and ye cannot bear all things now; nevertheless, be of good cheer, for I will lead you along. The kingdom is yours and the blessings thereof are yours, and the riches of eternity are yours" (D&C 78:17–18).

Keep your eternal focus, endure to the end, and you will experience great things to come.

CHAPTER 22

What Will Happen to the Governments of the Earth?

ave you ever thought about what would happen if you became president of the United States? Think about how much fun you would have! You could drive around in a limousine with hundreds of secret service men protecting you. You could invite all of your friends up to the White House for pizza and a movie. You could ride around in Air Force One, the president's personal jet. You could plan all of your meetings in Hawaii.

Being president, though, wouldn't always be fun. The responsibilities you'd have would make the job tough. You'd have to keep a budget, work with the Congress and the Senate, and make important decisions, like whether to go to war and how many troops to send. Being president sounds like a lot of fun until you think about it.

All presidents or prime ministers have difficult jobs, and all nations have difficult challenges. War might ravage one, while economic depression or famine might plague another. As you think about all of the nations of the world and the many challenges they face, it seems overwhelming. With so many important decisions facing them, presidents are bound to make mistakes. Some of those mistakes lead to the suffering of their people or even to the suffering of people in other nations. Wouldn't it be nice to have a wise leader who could help all of the world's leaders make good choices for their people? I don't think that day is too far off.

What will happen to world governments when Christ comes? Remember, a lot of good people will inherit the paradisiacal earth when he arrives, many of them not members of the Church. So we'll still need someone to guide us and govern the world. Who will that be? The tenth article of faith says, "Christ will reign personally upon the earth." That means that when he comes again he will be our king and lawgiver. He will come in power and glory to rule the nations of the earth.

Elder Bruce R. McConkie wrote, "As the King of the whole earth, [Jesus Christ] shall make a full end of all nations, and they, combining under one head, shall become the kingdom of our God and of his Christ, and he shall reign forever and ever. There will be no law but his law when he comes, and he shall restore his judges and rulers as at the first" (A New Witness, 642).

Can you imagine what our world will be like when Christ comes to reign? What will it be like having a perfect being, a God, leading and teaching and governing all nations of the earth? What an incredible experience that will be. Will there be war? No. Will there be contention? No. Will there be droughts and famine and starvation? No. Will you get to ride in Air Force One with all of your friends? I don't know. But I do know that there will be great peace and joy as Christ takes his rightful place as king of kings. The world has suffered much at the hand of unrighteous people hungry for power and authority (D&C 98:9). It will be a welcome day when Christ comes to assume his rightful place as leader of the world, displacing Satan and his wicked followers.

So what will happen to national governments? Will they be destroyed or disbanded? Will they continue? Joseph Fielding Smith taught: "When our Savior comes to rule in the millennium, *all governments will become subject unto his government,* and this has been referred to as the kingdom of God, which it is; but this is the *political kingdom which will embrace all people whether they are in the Church or not*" (*Doctrines of Salvation,* 1:229; emphasis added). This means that there will be many governments at the time Christ comes to earth. They will still have their own leaders, but Christ will rule over them, and they will learn from his counsel.

If we remain righteous, I imagine we'll have an opportunity to see this great event take place—whether we're alive or not when he comes. (I'll explain more about that in the next chapter.) That brings up another point about how the governments of the earth will be run. The Prophet Joseph Smith taught that many righteous Saints will help Christ govern the world. He said, "Christ and the resurrected Saints will reign over the earth during the thousand years" of the Millennium (*Teachings,* 421). Can you see Captain Moroni being one of the resurrected beings who's in charge of helping a nation live righteously? Wouldn't it be a privilege to be with him and many other great resurrected Saints as they follow the direction of the Lord, helping the nations of the earth govern themselves in righteousness. That day will come, and you and I may see it.

When that great council meeting takes place at Adam-ondi-Ahman, much more will happen besides the administration of the sacrament. At that time Christ will take his rightful place as king of kings. He will be crowned the leader and ruler of the world, "holding the keys of the universe" (Smith, *Teachings,* 157). I hope all of us look forward to the day when Christ comes and brings with him perfect leadership, peace, and perfect love for all people.

When Christ comes to be our king, it will be a day like no other.

There will be no election campaign. There will be no long debates or speeches. Rather, those at Adam-ondi-Ahman will raise their right hands and unanimously sustain Christ, showing that they will follow him and do what he asks.

It will be an awesome day.

Chapter 23

What Will Happen to the Dead?

Some of the most frightening movies of all times have to do with dead people—usually those who, by some amazing power or force, decide to come alive again and haunt the living or take over their bodies or something like that. Dead people have always fascinated the world. Every culture is curious about death and what happens to those who have passed on. Even here in the United States, we celebrate spooky things associated with death. On Halloween we go to haunted houses and, almost literally, get scared to death when people in costumes come after us with chain saws and all kinds of other nasty things.

The good thing about all the craziness and fun at Halloween is that we, as members of The Church of Jesus Christ of Latter-day Saints, know true doctrine about the dead. We know and understand that there is a place where all the spirits go who have passed on. It's called the spirit world. It's not a scary place or a place where spirits take a short break before they return to earth to terrify those still living. It's a peaceful place for the righteous as they await the resurrection, but it's a miserable place for those who wish they had been more righteous on earth.

People in the Philippines, where I served my mission, celebrate something similar to Halloween. It's called All Souls Day. Families pack a big meal, gather a few games, rehearse some fun stories to tell and then go to the grave site of a deceased loved one. Once there, they socialize, eat, and play games on the grave or by the tombstone of their great-grandma or some other relative! Best of all, families remember relatives and tell stories about them.

As Latter-day Saints, we know that our loved ones and all others who have died are waiting for the Second Coming and for Christ to bring peace to the world. But what will happen to the dead during the Second Coming? A few chapters ago we talked about three different kinds of people: celestial, terrestrial, and telestial. Now let's find out what will happen to each group when Christ comes again.

Celestial Dead

The celestial dead are righteous Saints who lived good lives and served the Lord with all their "heart, might, mind, and strength" (D&C 4:2). If you were going to celebrate All Souls Day, you would bring the best food to their grave sites—steak and potatoes, with ice cream and cake for dessert! These people sacrificed all they had for God and are looking forward to their resurrection. They kept their covenants and will be blessed for their obedience. The Lord has told us that the celestial dead will be resurrected first. An angel will blow his "trump," and then "they who have slept in their graves shall come forth, . . . and they also shall be caught up to meet him in the midst of the pillar of heaven—they are Christ's, the first fruits, they who shall descend with him first" (D&C 88:97–98).

Terrestrial Dead

After a second angel sounds his trumpet, those who lived good lives but were deceived by the craftiness of men or who rejected the gospel in this life will be resurrected. They did not have valiant testimonies of Jesus. After the resurrection of the celestial dead, the terrestrial dead will arise from their graves to be judged of their works. You would bring soup and sandwiches to their graves—an okay meal but not the best. The Second Coming will be a day of rejoicing for them because of their resurrection, but it will also be a day of sad reflection because they could have done better while living on the earth.

Telestial Dead

A third trumpeter will come forth and blow his horn but not until a thousand years after the first two. After the celestial and terrestrial dead are resurrected, the "spirits of men who are . . . under condemnation" will have to wait until the end of the Millennium before their turn comes (D&C 88:100–101). It will be a long waiting period for them because they will be stuck in spirit prison until then. Remember, they are murderers, adulterers, and those who love to lie. After the Second Coming, they will have a thousand years to sit around thinking about what they did wrong. For All Souls Day, they would get gristly pork and moldy cheese, along with lima beans for dessert!

As you can tell, the Second Coming will be an awesome day for the righteous and an unpleasant day for the unrighteous. For the unrighteous it will be like waiting in line for hours for something you really want. Then, just as you get to the counter, the store closes and you have to come back the next day—or, in this case, in a thousand years.

Do you understand why our resurrection is so important? The Lord tells us why. He said, "For man is spirit. The elements are eternal, and spirit and element, inseparably connected, receive a fulness of joy; and *when separated, man cannot receive a fulness of joy*" (D&C 93:33–34;

emphasis added). If our bodies and spirits are not reunited, we cannot be completely happy. Concerning the resurrection, the Lord also said, "The spirit and the body [will] be united never again to be divided, *that they might receive a fulness of joy*" (D&C 138:17; emphasis added). I believe that most of us will be on our knees—once we have our bodies again—in gratitude to God for the miracle of the resurrection.

We can't end this chapter without taking a look at one more important principle. We just learned that the dead, including us, will be resurrected either at the coming of Christ or later. We must not forget who made resurrection possible.

Three days after the death of Jesus Christ, Mary Magdalene came to his tomb. Frustrated because the stone had been rolled away and thinking that someone had taken the Savior's body, Mary began to weep. At that moment she heard a gentle voice: "Woman, why weepest thou?" Mary, thinking it was the gardener, asked where he had taken Jesus. Jesus then called her by name: "Mary." Through tears, Mary recognized Jesus and responded with respect and love: "Master" (John 20:15–16).

Because of Jesus, we will be resurrected. Because of Jesus, our spirits and bodies will be reunited. Because of Jesus, we will enjoy eternal life. Just as Mary had the opportunity to see the Savior and witness that he was a resurrected being, we too, through the power of the Spirit, can receive that same witness.

May we always thank our Heavenly Father for the gift of his son. May we show gratitude for the gift of immortality. May we someday, as did Mary, have the opportunity to look into the Savior's eyes and with love call out, "Master."

CHAPTER 24

What Will Happen to Satan?

Have you ever heard the phrase "mission statement"? A mission statement is a statement written by an organization that gives a clear idea of what that organization is all about. The Articles of Faith can be considered our mission statement as Latter-day Saints. Even God has a mission statement. It's found in Moses 1:39: "For behold, this is my work and my glory—to bring to pass the immortality and eternal life of man." In other words, God's desire and main goal is to help all of his children become like him. He wants each of us to enjoy the life he enjoys. He sounds like a loving father to me.

Well, what about Satan? What do you think his mission statement is? How about, "Behold, this is my work and my disgrace—to bring to pass the spiritual destruction and misery of all of God's children. And I'll enjoy it too." He wants nothing more than to make us just as miserable as he is (2 Nephi 2:27). He spends all of his energy and time trying to succeed at that mission. He enjoys the misery we suffer in this life. He even laughs with his angels when we make poor choices (Moses 7:26). Can you imagine working for such a guy? It would be horrible!

Now that we understand a little about Satan and his goals, let's take a look at what will happen to him when Christ comes. The scriptures teach us that Satan will be "bound" at the Second Coming (D&C 88:110). Not only that, but he'll be cast into a "bottomless pit" (Revelation 20:3). Cool, but what does that mean? When I think of Satan being bound, I think of him being wrapped up with ropes and chains so there's no way he can get out of his cell. But that's not exactly what will happen.

Being "bound" and cast into a "bottomless pit" are symbolic. I can't quite conceive of steel chains or pits that could hold Satan. The only power I know of that will bind Satan or render him powerless is righteous living. Nephi agreed. He said, "Because of the righteousness of his people, Satan has no power" (1 Nephi 22:26). Eldred G. Smith, patriarch to the Church, added, "The war that started in heaven has not ended yet and shall not end until everyone has proved the extent of his ability to resist Satan. Even Jesus Christ had to bind Satan when he was tempted in the wilderness. Satan had no power over him, because Jesus resisted his temptations. Then the record says, '. . . he departed from him for a season' (Luke 4:13)" (in Conference Report, April 1970, 142).

So it's not ropes and chains that will bind Satan. When Christ comes, Satan will be bound by our righteous living. He won't be able to do anything but sit home and knit. What a boring time for him— nothing to do but wish he were out wreaking havoc somewhere. Are there other ways Satan will be bound?

The scriptures say, "And in that day Satan shall not have power to tempt any man" (D&C 101:28). It sounds like there are actually two things that will bind Satan: the righteousness of the Saints and the power of God. President George Q. Cannon said, "We talk about Satan being bound. *Satan will be bound by the power of God; but he will be bound also by the determination of the people of God not to listen to him, not to be governed by him* (Gospel Truth, 1:68; emphasis added; 2 Nephi 30:18; Ether 8:26).

Can you imagine being grounded for a thousand years? That's how long Satan will be bound. You think it's bad when your parents ground you for a day or two or even a week. Well, whine no more. We just discovered the ultimate grounding—a thousand years!

For the righteous, however, the thousand years of the Savior's personal reign on earth will be a time of incredible joy, peace, and harmony. Think how great it will be to live in a world without sin, bad thoughts, or even bad desires. It will be wonderful!

Eventually, Satan will be off grounding. He'll be so angry after being out of action for a thousand years that he'll be back with a vengeance, causing major problems. Actually, he'll cause a war—the final battle between good and evil. It will be Satan and his followers against Michael, or Adam, and his followers.

"And then he shall be loosed for a little season, that he may gather together his armies. And Michael . . . shall gather together his armies, even the hosts of heaven. And the devil shall gather together his armies; even the hosts of hell, and shall come up to battle against Michael and his armies" (D&C 88:111–13).

Now don't worry; we already know who'll win. (I wonder if the battle will be on ESPN.) "And then cometh the battle of the great God; and the devil and his armies shall be cast away into their own place, that they shall not have power over the saints any more at all" (D&C 88:114). I often think how awesome it would be to fight with Adam on one side of you and Captain Moroni on the other side. And what would it be like to have the hosts of heaven, including the two thousand stripling warriors, to back you up? Trust me, you wouldn't lose.

You know what the most interesting thing about this chapter is? We actually have power to bind Satan now. We can kick him out of our lives, if we choose to, by making good choices. The more righteous we are, the less influence he has in our lives.

Let's start the grounding now! Make a choice to bind Satan through righteous living. Later on we'll talk more about how to do that.

CHAPTER 25

What Will Happen after Christ Comes?

There's only one way to appreciate the coming changes. Take a ride into the future! So keep your hands and feet inside at all times and hold on tight. We're boarding the Millennial Train! What's the Millennial Train? It's a ride that takes you into the thousand-year period following the Second Coming. Picture yourself riding on a train, taking an awesome tour of the most incredible country you've ever seen. Along the way you'll make several stops to check out the scenery. The stops will be quick, but you'll get a glimpse of some great things. There's a lot to learn and look forward to. Ready? Here we go!

Stop No. 1—Millennial Quick Facts: When Christ comes again in his glory, it will be the beginning of a time we know as the Millennium. The Millennium will last a thousand years. It will be a time of joy and excitement (D&C 29:11).

Stop No. 2—Twinklage: There won't be any death as we know it after Christ comes. As discussed earlier, people will live until they're a hundred years old. Then they'll be changed in moment to a resurrected being. It'll be great! No waiting around in the spirit world. Just blink your eyes and go from death to a resurrected being (D&C 43:32; Isaiah 65:20). A *twinklage* is a resurrected person, though you won't find that word in the scriptures. (I made it up.)

Stop No. 3—Tri-city: Three major cities will be on the earth during the Millennium. Other cities will be here on earth, but the three main places will be the capital cities of the Lord: Jerusalem in the Middle East, the New Jerusalem in Missouri, and the City of Enoch, which will come down from heaven to the earth. From these three cities the Lord will govern the world.

Stop No. 4—The Millennial Zoo: The Millennial Zoo will be a great place to go because there won't be any bars or cages. You'll get to walk right up to a lion and pet him. Gorillas will roam free, and you'll get to pet them too. They'll even like it! Animals won't be mean to each other, and we won't be mean to them. Dogs and cats will live together in peace, and hunters will have to take up a new sport. All animals will be as they were in the Garden of Eden (D&C 101:26; Orson Pratt, in *Journal of Discourses*, 20:18).

Stop No. 5—Missionary Madness: Missionary work will be highly successful. There will be many good people living on the earth ready to accept the gospel, so missionaries will be needed until every person has been baptized and accepted the truth. I wonder what the mission will be called? Maybe the City of Enoch Mission or the Millennial Mission. The monthly baptisms will be incredible (Smith, *Answers to Gospel Questions*, 1:108, 110–11).

Stop No. 6—Life as Usual: Many things will be normal during the Millennium. People will get married and have children. They'll plant crops and harvest crops. Businesses will grow, new cities will be built, and people will be educated. Everyone will learn the same "pure" language so that no one will be confused (McConkie, *Mormon Doctrine*, 496–97; Zephaniah 3:9).

Stop No. 7—No More Wishing: Whatever you ask for during the Millennium, you'll get! (D&C 101:27). Can you imagine getting everything you ever wanted? Cars, planes, vacations, money will all be ours! Yes! (Sorry, I got a little carried away.) Actually, during the Millennium people will be so righteous that they won't ask for unrighteous things. However, everything good will be given to them. We often have a tendency to pray for things we shouldn't, but during the Millennium we'll pray for the right things.

Stop No. 8—An Awesome Hymn: During the Millennium we'll sing a new hymn. Its lyrics are found in Doctrine and Covenants 84:99–102. It's a song of praise to God for all the great things he has done for us. It's about the binding of Satan and the presence of God in the midst of his people. Turn to your scriptures and read all of the words of this great millennial hymn.

Stop No. 9—Temple Work: During this thousand-year period, temple work will go forward like never before. Temples will be everywhere. I'll bet that temples will be open twenty-four hours a day—except for Sunday and Monday evenings, of course. Can you imagine doing baptisms for the dead all day and night for a thousand years? It'll be cool. Heavenly beings will even assist with this great undertaking (Smith, *Doctrines of Salvation*, 2:252).

Stop No. 10—A Time Like No Other: Elder Orson Pratt said, "What a happy earth this creation will be, when this purifying process shall come, and the earth be filled with the knowledge of God as the waters cover the great deep! What a change! Travel, then, from one end of the earth to another, you can find no wicked man, no drunken man, no man to blaspheme the name of the Great Creator, no one to lay hold on his neighbor's goods, and steal them, no one to commit whoredoms" (in *Journal of Discourses*, 21:325).

I hope your ride on the Millennial Train has been a good one. I also hope that you've had a chance to reflect on how great God is. All this will be made possible because of him, for he is the train's engineer. So when the time comes to board for real, I hope you'll be ready for an exciting ride. It'll be a ride you'll never forget!

PART FOUR

Preparing for the Second Coming

CHAPTER 26

Stand in Holy Places

To prepare for the coming of the Lord, the Lord has counseled us, "Wherefore, stand ye in holy places, and be not moved, until the day of the Lord come; for behold, it cometh quickly, saith the Lord" (D&C 87:8).

The first chapter of this book mentions a young woman who was terrified of the Second Coming. Her biggest fear was that flies would get her, so she wanted to go someplace safe where she could get away from them. Well, I hope I've made it clear that the horrible events that are to come are reserved for the wicked. The righteous will be affected to some degree by the coming events, but there's no promise of safety at all for the wicked.

As we prepare for the Second Coming, many of us want to know what to do to prepare for that day. And just like my student, we'll need to find safe places where we can go to find protection. But where are those places? Will we be able to get there in time? Let's answer those questions.

Last year my oldest daughter, Amber, turned twelve. She was so excited to finally graduate from Primary and go into the Young Women program. But the thing she was most excited about was the opportunity to go to the temple for the first time. My wife and I decided we would take her to the temple for her birthday to do baptisms for the dead. When the special day came, we dressed up and made our way to the Mount Timpanogos Utah Temple in American Fork. We had a great time together. Amber was nervous but felt the Spirit of the Lord.

While we were there, we met a young woman in her twenties. She and a friend were also doing baptisms for the dead. She was kind and took a few minutes to share a personal story with our daughter. She said she had had a hard time in high school. She didn't have a lot of friends and struggled with the atmosphere at her school. One day she had an idea. She would go to the temple once a week to do baptisms for the dead. And she did. For the last two years of high school, she went to the temple every week.

After sharing her story, she bore her testimony to my daughter. "Coming to the temple during that challenging time gave me courage to endure," she said. We were grateful that she took the time to share that experience with us.

You too can prepare for the challenges to come by going to the holiest place on earth—the temple. Just because you're young doesn't mean you can't go. Get a temple recommend from your bishop and attend the temple as often as you can. In the temple you'll find peace and the courage you need to face life's challenges.

President Ezra Taft Benson said, "In the peace of these lovely temples, sometimes we find solutions to the serious problems of life. Under the influence of the Spirit, sometimes pure knowledge flows to us there. Temples are places of personal revelation. When I have been weighted down by a problem or a difficulty, I have gone to the house of the Lord with a prayer in my heart for answers. These answers have come in clear and unmistakable ways" ("What I Hope You Will Teach Your Children about the Temple," *Ensign*, August 1985, 8).

There are other holy places where we can stand, including our homes. Our homes can also help prepare us for the Second Coming. Look what the Bible Dictionary says about homes: "[The temple] is the most holy of any place of worship on earth. *Only the home can compare with the temple in sacredness*" (781; emphasis added).

Homes can be places where we find strength and courage. Homes are where family prayers are given, family home evening is held, and blessings are given to children. Just having the priesthood in your home can be a blessing. Allowing your father to give you a blessing when you need one can bring peace to your life and help you find answers to your prayers.

So what if you live in a home where these things don't occur? You can still encourage your parents to do righteous things, and you can offer to give a home evening lesson yourself or encourage your family to have prayer together. You can work hard to limit contention, obey your parents, and live in such a way that the Spirit will come and dwell there because you are doing your best. Making your home like a temple can be hard work, but it's worth it to create another holy place where you can stand.

What about Church? Obviously, Church can be a holy place too—provided you make it one. Let's suppose you're out late Saturday night on a date. Because you don't get up on time the next morning, you have to rush around trying to find your clothes and scriptures. In your rush you get irritated with other family members. Then you wolf down your breakfast and run out the door, hoping to get to Church on time. Is it worth it, or are you better off sleeping in and skipping Church?

Of course it's worth it. We go to Church for several good reasons. We go to learn gospel principles, be with our friends and neighbors, think about good things, sing, and pray. But as important as those things are, they're not the primary reason we go. We go primarily to partake of the sacrament, renew our covenants, and remember the Savior. As we partake of the sacrament, we can be forgiven of our sins and receive the blessing of having the Spirit with us always—not just on Sunday. We need the Holy Ghost in our lives. When he is with us constantly, we're better able to make good choices that will prepare us for the Second Coming.

What about association with friends? Can being in their presence be like standing in a holy place? Yes, if we have the right friends. We usually become like our friends, so if our friends have good attitudes about the gospel and are trying to do what's right, they can be a great blessing to us. On the other hand, if our friends are negative about spiritual things and mock the Lord and his Church, we may want to find other friends.

Remember, there's only one person responsible to prepare you for the Second Coming, and that's you. Don't take a chance on having unrighteous friends and still think you'll be all right. Peer pressure is a powerful tool Satan can use against you.

"Choose your friends carefully," the *For the Strength of Youth* pamphlet tells us. "They will greatly influence how you think and act, and even help determine the person you will become. Choose friends who share your values so you can strengthen and encourage each other in living high standards. A true friend will encourage you to be your best self" (12).

The last holy place isn't a building or a place or a friend. It's you. Your own life can be a holy place. As you keep yourself free from sin and remain humble enough to repent when you make mistakes, the Lord will bless you, and you will find great satisfaction in knowing that you are prepared for his coming. One of my favorite scriptures tells us how to make our lives a holy place.

"Organize yourselves; prepare every needful thing; and establish a *life,* even a *life* of prayer, a *life* of fasting, a *life* of faith, a *life* of learning, a *life* of glory, a *life* of order, a *life* of God" (D&C 88:119; emphasis added). Okay, I replaced the word "house" with "life," but think about that scripture. Your life can be a holy place. By focusing on simple things like prayer and fasting, you can prepare for the Lord to come. Great personal protection comes from living a godly life.

The scriptures tell us to stand in holy places and not be moved. Part of creating a holy place is standing up for what we believe. Though the world may pressure you to change your values and beliefs, stand up for what you know is right. Don't allow yourself to be moved by what's wrong, even if it's popular or cool. I know you can do it!

Chapter 27

Plenty of Oil

One of my favorite stories is the parable of the ten virgins. In this parable ten women take oil lamps with them as they go to meet the bridegroom. Here's the deal: They don't know when he's coming. That's why they take oil lamps with them. If he comes at night, they'll be ready to follow the marriage procession to the wedding and wedding feast.

Matthew tells us that five of the virgins were wise and five were foolish. What made five of them foolish? Even though they took their lamps with them, they didn't take any oil. The virgins who were wise, on the other hand, took "oil in their vessels with their lamps" (Matthew 25:4).

Well, it got to be late and everyone fell asleep as they were waiting for the groom. At midnight someone started yelling that the groom was finally coming. When the virgins awoke, they realized in the darkness that they had to light their lamps. The five foolish virgins, of course, didn't have any oil, so they did what made sense. They asked the other virgins for some of their oil.

You might think that if the wise virgins had been righteous they would have given some oil to the foolish virgins. But nooooo! They refused to share. Instead, they told their foolish friends to go buy their own oil—even though it was midnight. How selfish!

While the foolish virgins ran off to look for an open store, the groom came. Those who were ready and waiting for him went with him to the marriage. After they arrived, "the door was shut." When the foolish virgins finally arrived with oil in their lamps, they began banging on the door and calling out, "Lord, Lord, open to us!" Then came a voice from inside the door. It was the groom! But instead of opening the door for the foolish five, as they excitedly expected, he told them, "I know you not" (Matthew 25:10–12).

At first it might seem that this story is merely about five forgetful virgins and five selfish virgins. I was always taught to share, and it only seems right that the five prepared virgins share with the others. I'm sure you would have shared your oil, right? But wait a minute! This is not just a story about ten virgins, oil, and a wedding. It's a parable about the Second Coming. The ten virgins represent members of the Church, and the groom represents Christ. In the last verse of the parable, the Lord says, "Watch therefore, for ye know neither the day nor the hour wherein the Son of man cometh" (Matthew 25:13).

The oil in the parable is our testimonies. The wise virgins couldn't give away their oil when the groom came for the same reason you won't be able to give away your testimony to someone else—or receive a testimony from someone else—when Christ comes again. If you don't have a testimony when Christ comes, there will be no getting one. It will be too late. The door will be shut, and you will not be allowed to enter. In other words, now is the time to develop and strengthen your testimony.

Now is the time to put plenty of oil in your lamp so that you can be ready when he comes.

Turns out the five wise virgins weren't selfish after all. They just couldn't give away something that others have to work for on their own. The years you spend reading the scriptures every day, the thousands of prayers you say, the hundreds of Church meetings and seminary classes you attend, the countless hours of service you give, and the mission you serve can't be given to someone who never does those things. Your testimony is yours. You earned it. You can bear it, but you can't give away what has become a part of you through sacrifice and hard work. And neither could the five wise virgins.

So how do we develop testimonies? Drop by drop. You can't fill your lamp all at once. You must work on filling it every day by living the gospel, following the prophet and other Church leaders, serving others, sacrificing, and enduring. It's the small things that fill an oil lamp with oil. We all have different amounts of oil in our lamps. A few examples of testimonies follow. Find out where you are, and determine to improve on what you already have.

One-Drop Testimony: This testimony is based on the testimony of others. You believe because your parents believe. That's not such a bad thing to begin with, but remember that when Christ comes you will need your own. Often people are satisfied with one drop because they don't want to make the effort to change and improve. Change can be difficult, and some are not willing to add more oil to their lamp. They go to Church because they have to, or they go to Young Men or Young Women meetings because there's nothing else to do. Sometimes they don't go at all. One-droppers usually don't serve in the Church unless forced by parents or coerced by leaders. When the Groom comes, one drop will not provide sufficient light to make it through the darkness.

Teaspoon Testimony: Composed of a little more than just one drop, this testimony is based on fun. In other words, if Sunday School is fun and my teacher brings doughnuts, my testimony is good. If my seminary teacher is exciting and has a good sense of humor, then I'll believe. If we go boating, hiking, or skydiving, or take the shuttle to the moon for Young Men and Young Women activities, then the Church must be true. But once things get boring, my faith dwindles and my testimony weakens. If Church isn't fun and there's no one to entertain me, I'm outta here.

Having fun in Church is great, but you can squeeze only so much oil out of being entertained. Teaspoon Testimonies don't last. Those who have them will end up searching for more oil when Christ comes again.

Half-empty, Half-full Testimony: A lot more than a teaspoon, this testimony is based on your positive or negative attitude about life and the Church. If you don't like the bishop because he doesn't say hello every Sunday, your testimony's half-empty. If your bishop caters to your every need, your testimony's half-full. If you feel that everyone loves and accepts you, you're good to go. But once you begin to doubt that you're accepted, there goes your testimony. The frightening thing about this testimony is that it's based on perception—your perception.

This testimony is also based on the direction your family is going. If your mom and dad are active in the Church, so are you. If your parents are inactive and don't read the scriptures or pray, neither do you. If life is not going well and you're stressed out, your testimony becomes stressed out, and you doubt some of your beliefs.

A Half-full, Half-empty Testimony is shaky because life has its ups and downs, and people are inconsistent in how they communicate, feel, and act. You don't want to be a testimony chameleon—changing your testimony with your environment. A half-full or half-empty lamp will only get you halfway to Christ.

Overflowing Testimony: This is the kind of testimony the five wise virgins had. They were prepared, and no one could take away their oil.

An Overflowing Testimony is one that is based on the Lord Jesus Christ. It comes by doing what the Lord has asked of you. It comes from prayer and fasting, scripture reading, and regular attendance at Church. It comes through the power of the Holy Ghost, who has born witness to your spirit that Christ lives and that the Church has been restored.

If you have an Overflowing Testimony, you don't need to be forced to do what's right. You just do it. If life is hard and you're experiencing stress, you go to your faith for strength. If your parents aren't doing what's right, you do what's right anyway. If the bishop doesn't say hello, you understand that he's a busy man with a lot to worry about. Your testimony is strong because you know Christ lives and loves you. He is your rock. When you're invited to the wedding and feast, your lamp will be burning brightly.

How's your testimony? If it's weak, I challenge you to strengthen it. I know you can. But keep in mind that you'll have to work for it, and you'll be tested. Don't be discouraged. You can succeed. With patience and faith, you can be ready for the Second Coming.

Remember, you can't fill your lamp all at once. Just one drop at a time is all the Lord requires. Start today, and your lamp will have plenty of oil when Christ comes.

CHAPTER 28

Take the Holy Spirit As Your Guide

I n the Doctrine and Covenants, the Lord expounds upon the parable of the ten virgins. He said, "And at that day, when I shall come in my glory, shall the parable be fulfilled which I spake concerning the ten virgins. For they that are wise and have received the truth, and have taken the Holy Spirit for their guide, and have not been deceived—verily I say unto you, they shall not be hewn down and cast into the fire, but shall abide the day" (D&C 45:56–57).

Whoa! We just read the Lord's description of the wise virgins. They are those who receive the truth, take the Holy Spirit as their guide, and are not deceived.

So how do you and I become wise as we prepare for the Second Coming? First, we must accept the truth when we hear it. A few years ago President Gordon B. Hinckley told the young women of the Church, "You do not need to drape rings up and down your ears. One modest pair of earrings is sufficient" ("A Prophet's Counsel and Prayer for Youth," *Ensign*, January 2001, 7). The next day in seminary, some of the young women and young men were upset at what the prophet said. They said earrings just weren't that big of a deal. They refused to obey the prophet of the Lord or accept the truth of his words.

Later in class that day, as I welcomed a sister with long blond hair, I asked her if she had heard President Hinckley's talk. She said she had. I then asked her what she thought of his remarks. Without hesitation she pulled her hair away from her ears. Where she used to wear two pairs of earrings she now only wore one pair. She looked up and asked, "Does that answer your question?" Here was a young woman who had received the truth and obeyed. Other students responded the same way, stating that they didn't realize that's how the prophet felt. They received the truth and obeyed. I wanted to jump up and down and shout for joy at their response, but I controlled myself until I got home.

In addition to receiving the truth, the wise virgins took the Holy Spirit as their guide. Think for a moment what a guide does. If you have ever been river rafting, you know. He takes you down the raging river safely. He knows the dangerous spots that could capsize the raft or trap it in a current. He tells you the rules of river rafting and what to do if problems occur. If you don't listen to his instructions, you could end up getting hurt or jeopardizing someone else. But if you listen and obey, you can have a great experience.

Listening to the Spirit is like listening to a river guide. Listen to the Spirit, and you'll be safe and ready for the Lord to come. Ignore what he says, and you'll be unprepared for that day. But how do you know if you're listening to the Spirit? How do you know if you're taking the Spirit as your guide? To answer those questions, let's explore how the Spirit works. We learn the first great thing about the Holy Ghost from an Old Testament prophet named Elijah.

Elijah was being hunted by a ferocious queen who wanted to kill him. He was terrified and came to the Lord in prayer for help. The Lord then sent him up Mount Horeb, also known as Sinai. On the mountain, "a great and strong wind" arose. The wind was so strong it broke rocks in pieces. Poor Elijah probably had to hold on to a tree as tight as he could. Next, a massive earthquake shook the ground, likely knocking Elijah off his feet. Then came a huge fire. Can you imagine going through those experiences?

The best part came next. The scripture says, "And after the fire a still small voice" (1 Kings 19:11–12). So why did Elijah have to go through the wind, the earthquake, and the fire? Maybe to teach him how quiet and still the Lord's voice can be in comparison to events in our lives that are loud and overbearing.

We learn from Elijah's experience that the Holy Ghost does not usually communicate through loud experiences but rather through quiet experiences that require us to listen carefully. We may miss the Spirit's message if we're not listening or paying attention. If we believe that the Holy Ghost communicates only in loud, overwhelming ways, we may be listening to the wrong voice.

President Howard W. Hunter said, "I get concerned when it appears that strong emotion or free-flowing tears are equated with the presence of the Spirit. Certainly the Spirit of the Lord can bring strong emotional feelings, including tears, but that outward manifestation ought not to be confused with the presence of the Spirit itself" (*The Teachings of Howard W. Hunter*, 184).

Taking the Spirit as our guide means that we are willing to take the time to listen. If our lives are so busy that we don't take time to ponder and pray, we may not hear the Holy Ghost. If we're always listening to loud music or loud television programs or loud movies, how can we hear and understand the still, small voice? Even the Nephites in the Book of Mormon had trouble understanding God's voice to them. On one occasion they had to hear the Father's voice three times before they understood it (3 Nephi 11:3–7).

In the last days Satan will do everything in his power to make things louder and more confusing. He wants to prevent us from listening to the still, small voice. He wants us to be foolish virgins who are not prepared when the Groom comes. Unfortunately, he will succeed in preventing many from following the guide of the Holy Spirit.

Speaking of the ten virgins, Elder Dallin H. Oaks said, "The arithmetic of this parable is chilling. The ten virgins obviously represent members of Christ's Church, for all were invited to the wedding feast and all knew what was required to be admitted when the bridegroom came. But only half were ready when he came" ("Preparation for the Second Coming," *Ensign*, May 2004, 8).

And how will Satan prevent half of the members of the Church from being prepared? We know that one of his tactics is to make it difficult for us to hear the Holy Ghost. But we must fight back. If we're going to be ready, we must make every effort to prepare ourselves by turning down the music, turning off the television, and tuning in the Spirit. We must spend time not only reading the scriptures but also pondering them. What would have happened if Joseph Smith hadn't been listening when he read James 1:5? He would not have been prepared to pray for an answer.

We must be like Joseph and make time to be close to the Lord and become familiar with his voice. If we do, the Holy Spirit will become our guide as we travel down the river called the "last days"—the river that will eventually lead us to the presence of the Lord.

Listen. He may be speaking even now. I promise that if you are still, you will hear him.

CHAPTER 29

One-Tenth

One of the most interesting stories regarding tithing is found in the book of Acts. It's a story about a man named Ananias and his wife, Sapphira. They decided to sell some land for one reason or another and afterward agreed privately not to tell anyone how much they got for it. Thinking they were pretty tricky, Ananias brought their tithing to the prophet, who at the time was Peter. But rather than pay a full tithe, Ananias and Sapphira kept a portion for themselves. Peter, receiving revelation from the Lord, knew they owed more and asked Ananias why he wasn't paying a full tithing. Peter told Ananias that he had lied to God (Acts 5:1–4).

At that moment Ananias fell down dead in front of Peter. Apparently there was a Young Men's activity taking place that evening because several young men there took Ananias outside and buried him. About three hours later his wife arrived, not knowing what had happened. She was probably out shopping with the extra tithing money they had held back. Her husband never showed up, so she decided to look for him.

The moment she entered, Peter asked if it was true that they had sold their property for the price Ananias had quoted. She said yes, lying to Peter just as her husband had done. Then Peter looked her in the eye and said, "How is it that ye have agreed together to tempt the Spirit of the Lord? Behold, the feet of them which have buried thy husband are at the door, and shall carry thee out" (Acts 5:9).

The young men, who apparently had returned, may have sensed that Sapphira was about to meet the same fate as her husband. At that moment Sapphira fell down dead at the prophet's feet. The young men again entered, picked up the body, and buried her by her husband. Back then the young men had all kinds of interesting service projects!

You may be wondering why this story is so important. Well, it deals with the importance of paying tithing—not just paying it but honestly paying it. Ananias and Sapphira flunked the tithing test. They weren't honest with the Lord or the prophet. They thought they could pay just a portion and keep the rest for themselves. What a selfish way to think. But there's more to the story.

What happens to us today when we don't pay an honest tithe? We don't see young men waiting around the bishop's office so they can have the opportunity to bury someone. But something serious does happen. President Gordon B. Hinckley said, "In our time those found in dishonesty do not die as did Ananias and Sapphira, but something within them dies. Conscience chokes, character withers, self-respect vanishes, integrity dies" ("An Honest Man—God's Noblest Work,'" *Ensign*, May 1976, 61).

Paying an honest tithe is an important part of expressing how we feel about the Lord. When we're honest, the Lord recognizes our sacrifice and blesses us with his Spirit. Withholding all or part of our tithing deprives us of that blessing and other blessings the Lord desires to give us.

President Heber J. Grant said: "I appeal to the Latter-day Saints to be honest with the Lord and I promise them that peace, prosperity and financial success will attend those who are honest with our Heavenly Father. . . . When we set our heart upon the things of this world and fail to be strictly honest with the Lord we do not grow in the light and power and strength of the gospel as we otherwise would do" (in Conference Report, October 1929, 4–5).

As you can see, part of preparing for the Second Coming is being honest with the Lord regarding our tithes. But even more important than receiving spiritual strength and financial success, being honest in our tithes gives us protection.

I once heard of a family who had a beautiful home. They had lived there several years and enjoyed having a place of their own. One day they were driving home and saw smoke billowing in the sky. It was coming from their home. As they drove around the corner, they could see that their home was in flames. The fire department was desperately trying to put it out but with no success. Within a few hours, their home was nothing but a pile of smoking ash.

The family was devastated. They had lost everything, and although no one was hurt, all of their possessions were gone. The most frightening part of this story is that the couple didn't have fire insurance. They had no way to rebuild their home or recover financially from the fire.

I love this statement by Elder Marion G. Romney. He said, "The payment of tithing is also worthwhile as fire insurance" ("First Presidency Message Concerning Tithing," Ensign, June 1980, 3). The Lord has said, "He that is tithed shall not be burned at his coming" (D&C 64:23). Paying an honest tithing shows the Lord that we are willing to fill our lamps with oil and do what he asks of us. When the Lord comes again in his power and glory, those who have been honest with him will be spared.

The Old Testament prophet Malachi said, "Bring ye all the tithes into the storehouse, that there may be meat in mine house, and prove me now herewith, saith the Lord of hosts, if I will not open you the windows of heaven, and pour you out a blessing, that there shall not be room enough to receive it" (Malachi 3:10). But what about now? Does God bless us now for paying our tithing?

My wife and I had the opportunity to speak with Elder Jay Jensen of the Seventy when I was hired to work for the Church Educational System. We were quite nervous as we waited for our meeting, but our fears quickly dissolved when we met him. He was kind and friendly, and he put us at ease. He asked us many questions about our family and future, but he said one thing I will never forget. He told us that if we were faithful the Lord would pour out his blessings upon us.

Then he quoted Malachi 3:10 and asked us what blessings the Lord pours out upon faithful tithe payers. "Faith and wisdom," we answered. He then told us that when the Lord pours out blessings, he does miracles. He said the Lord would make the tires on our car last longer, the soles of our shoes travel farther, the food in our pantry go further, and many other simple things we might not notice.

I know that's what the Lord will do for you too. Not only will paying an honest tithe be good fire insurance, but it will also allow the Lord to bless you in ways you probably may not see. He will bless you with increased understanding as you study in school, he will give you courage when you are fearful, and he will guide you to make wise decisions.

What a blessing it is to pay tithing! Let's not become like Ananias and Sapphira. Let's be honest with the Lord as we give him his one-tenth and then watch as the windows of heaven open wide.

CHAPTER 30

No More Pride

Beware of pride, lest ye become as the Nephites of old," the Lord warns us (D&C 38:39). All through the Book of Mormon we see examples of how the Nephites destroyed themselves because of pride. We see similar examples of how pride destroyed people in the Old Testament. Cain, Saul, and even David were overcome by pride. Likewise, the New Testament shows us the pride of the Pharasees and Sadducees who opposed the Savior.

Pride's victims in the scriptures are long gone. But what about us today? Pride is all around us, although it is one of the most difficult sins to see. What is pride anyway? President Ezra Taft Benson told us that pride is enmity. He said, "*Enmity* means 'hatred toward, hostility to, or a state of opposition.' It is the power by which Satan wishes to reign over us" ("Beware of Pride," *Ensign*, May 1989, 4).

Satan will do anything he can to prevent us from being ready for the Second Coming. If he can tempt us to hate someone, be hostile toward someone, or oppose someone, then he causes us to sin. And those who sin aren't prepared for Christ's coming. If we are to really understand what pride is, we need to know that it all starts with enmity toward someone in some way. Knowing that enmity is the foundation of pride, it is easier for us to understand the three aspects of pride.

One aspect of pride is manifested by those who despise others for not having something they have. You know who I'm talking about. People who have this form of pride look down on others and mock them because they're not good enough in one way or another. It could be the football player with the big muscles who bullies other kids and picks on them. It could be the cheerleader who thinks that no one is as good looking or as talented as she is. It could be the trumpet player who thinks he's the best and is out to prove it. It could be the chess club member who thinks he's smarter than anyone else. It could be the Future Farmer of America who brags how great his show pig is, the bull rider who thinks he's the toughest guy in school, or the rich girl who thinks money makes her better than others. Without much regard for anyone else, these people seek to put themselves on top and will do anything to stay there. This form of pride is everywhere.

The next aspect of pride is the sin of being at the bottom and looking up with envy. Those with this kind of pride get angry at those who have talent or money or beauty. They backbite or gossip about them. They call them stuck-up because of their success or good fortune. Remember, this is enmity, a hatred for someone else. This aspect of pride is more common than looking down on others. President Benson said, "Pride is a sin that can readily be seen in others but is rarely admitted in ourselves" ("Beware of Pride," *Ensign*, May 1989, 4).

The last aspect of pride is not about looking down or looking up. It's about comparing yourself to others—wishing you had the same car or the same talent, wishing you had their money, parents, or friends. We call that envy.

The best thing we can do is love ourselves and those around us. If we are prideful in one of these three areas, we risk losing the Spirit. As a result, we find it difficult to be sensitive to the promptings of the Holy Ghost. Here's a silly poem I wrote that illustrates the three aspects of pride. See if you can find them.

The story is told of a bird
Her beautiful wings took her flight,
And when she would rest on the top of a tree,
She'd look down on society's plight.

His name was McGilvery Jones
He could not fly as you think,
For he was a skunk, and looking up at the bird
Stuck his nose in the air with a stink.

He came from the world down under,
A kangaroo who was hopping along
He noticed poor Jones with his nose in the air
And he said, "Oh, I have this all wrong"!

"I wish I could be like McGilvery,
With my nose upturned, then he blinked.
No cares in the world, I would be free,
With my tail in the air I would stink!"

But this could not be, as he looked up the tree
Wishing he had nice wings too.
Then the bird yelled back, with a squawk and a squack,
"You will just always be you."

So the bird flew away with an amazing glide,
McGilvery left the scene too.
And the kangaroo, not satisfied with himself,
Bowed his head and sobbed boohoo!

The moral of the story is this:
Looking down on others brings pain.
So does wanting to be someone you're not,
Like stinking and thinking you're incredibly hot.

So just be happy, whoever you are.
Don't try to be someone else,
Or make fun of others for who they've become.
The best you can be is yourself.

Take a minute to recover from that poem before you read on. Okay, so how do we overcome pride? President Benson said there's only one way: humility. We must humble ourselves. There are many ways we can do that. President Benson gives us a great list:

- Lifting others as high or higher than we are.
- Accepting counsel and chastisement.
- Rendering selfless service.
- Serving missions.
- Going to the temple more frequently.
- Confessing and forsaking our sins.
- Loving God, submitting our will to his, and putting him first in our lives.
- Humbling ourselves, repenting, and enduring to the end ("Beware of Pride," Ensign, May 1989, 7).

One of the hardest parts of being obedient is changing. But change is possible. I know we can change. I know that through the power of the Atonement, prayer, and hard work we can be humble. God will help us.

CHAPTER 31

Trust in the Lord

Moses was one of the greatest prophets in the Old Testament. He battled Pharaoh and, with God's help, sent plagues upon the Egyptians. The day finally came when Pharaoh couldn't take it anymore, and he let the Israelites go. Things went well until they came to the Red Sea. While standing on the beach, wondering what to do next, they felt the earth begin to shake. At first they may have thought it was an earthquake, but then they saw Pharaoh with his men and chariots coming after them.

Fear overcame them, and with wide eyes and gaping mouths, they did what many of them had learned to do best: they whined! As Pharaoh charged toward them, the people turned toward Moses and, freaking out, said, "Because there were no graves in Egypt, hast thou taken us away to die in the wilderness? Wherefore hast thou dealt thus with us, to carry us forth out of Egypt?" (Exodus 14:11).

Can you imagine? At the moment they needed help, instead of being patient and waiting for the Lord to work miracles, they whined.

They could have approached Moses and asked him what they could do. They could have started swimming across the Red Sea. They could have begun chucking chickens at Pharaoh and his army. But they complained instead. It was something they had perfected in Egypt.

How often in life do we do the same thing? When life gets a little tough, or things aren't going the way we think they should go, we murmur and complain, hoping that somehow through our whining things will get better. Or that someone will pay attention to us or feel bad for us.

So why did Israel complain? For the same reason we complain today. They didn't trust God.

Because the signs of the Second Coming are already taking place, we may start to become a little like the Israelites. "Oh no! What are we gonna do? We're all going to die!" I hope by this point you know that's not true. But like Israel, we may have a tendency to fall back on what we're familiar with when tough times come. How do I know? Well, when you have to do the dishes, do you whine and complain about it? When you have to mow the lawn, do you feel that the world has ended? When you have to do homework, do you complain?

Amidst today's wars and rumors of wars, do you do the same? Or do you have a quiet confidence in knowing that the prophesied signs are being fulfilled? When earthquakes shake your world and tidal waves wash upon you, will you run around (or swim around) wishing someone would stop them? Or do you understand the reason for these events, knowing that God is trying to get his rebellious children to repent?

When the Israelites came running to Moses, he had an incredible response. "Fear ye not, stand still [they must have been jumping up and down in a panicked frenzy], and see the salvation of the Lord. . . . The Lord shall fight for you, and ye shall hold your peace" (Exodus 14:13–14). In other words, Moses knew that the Lord would take care of them. Because they were doing what they had been commanded and were following God's prophet out of Egypt, Moses knew God would bless them. And he did.

In these last days it may seem that evil is winning. We hear the rumble of its influence coming in the distance. We see the chariots of wickedness racing ever closer through the media and the internet. We see the spears of Satan pointing directly at us. But we can fight back with faith, hope, and trust. Remember, God is in charge. It's up to us to fear not, stand still, and see the salvation of the Lord.

I love what the Lord told the Israelites to do next. He didn't part the Red Sea at first. He told Moses to command them to "go forward" (Exodus 14:15). Before God would do his great miracle, the Israelites had to step forward with faith. Then the miracle came. The angel of God stopped the Egyptians and the wind blew all night, parting the sea and clearing a path for the Israelites. Without further questions or complaints, the Israelites walked forward.

We need to understand that this is what God expects of us. Even though situations are difficult and life seems hard, we need to go forward so that God can work his miracles. Have a good attitude about things, speak positively of others, and serve the best you can. Change your negative thoughts to thoughts of faith. God will fight your battles for you, but you must be willing to show him that you trust him.

Another aspect of trusting in the Lord is enduring to the end. That sounds tough, like sitting through the ACT. Elder Henry B. Eyring said, "Simply enduring may seem almost beyond us. That's what the words in the scripture 'Ye must . . . endure to the end' seemed to mean to me when I first read them. It sounded grim, like sitting still and holding on to the arms of the chair while someone pulled out my tooth" ("In the Strength of the Lord," *Ensign*, May 2004, 17). I'm sure the Israelites felt that way as they wandered through the wilderness for forty years.

As we approach the Second Coming, we will see many people lose faith and endurance. They will give in to pornography or immorality without any thought of repentance. Remember that this life is a test, and the Lord wants to see if we will be worthy to be among those who are caught up to meet him when he comes again.

Elder Eyring continued: "The test a loving God has set before us is not to see if we can endure difficulty. It is to see if we can endure it well. We pass the test by showing that we remembered him and the commandments He gave us. And to endure well is to keep those commandments whatever the opposition, whatever the temptation, and whatever the tumult around us. We have that clear understanding because the restored gospel makes the plan of happiness so plain" ("In the Strength of the Lord," *Ensign*, May 2004, 17).

You can trust the Lord. You can faithfully endure to the end. God has given you the power to do so. He won't give you commandments you can't keep (1 Nephi 3:7). You must be positive even though life may be difficult.

I conclude this chapter with one of my favorite stories. Written by Tim Hansel, it's about being positive and trusting the Lord. It's called "The Road of Life."

At first, I saw God as my observer, my judge, keeping track of the things I did wrong, so as to know whether I merited heaven or hell when I die. He was out there sort of like a president.

But later on when I met Christ, it seemed as though life was rather like a bike ride, but it was a tandem bike, and I noticed that Christ was in the back helping me pedal.

I don't know just when it was that He suggested we change places, but life has not been the same since. When I had control, I knew the way. It was rather boring, but predictable. . . . It was the shortest distance between two points.

But when He took the lead, He knew delightful long cuts, up mountains and through rocky places at breakneck speeds, it was all I could do to hang on! Even though it looked like madness, He said, "Pedal!"

I worried and was anxious and asked, "Where are you taking me?" He laughed and didn't answer, and I started to learn to trust.

I forgot my boring life and entered into the adventure. And when I'd say, "I'm scared," He'd lean back and touch my hand.

He took me to people with gifts that I needed—gifts of healing, acceptance and joy. They gave me gifts to take on my journey, my Lord's and mine.

And we were off again. He said, "Give the gifts away; they're extra baggage, too much weight." So I did, to the people we met, and I found that in giving I received, and still our burden was light.

I did not trust Him, at first, in control of my life. I thought He'd wreck it; but He knows bike secrets, knows how to make it bend to take sharp corners, knows how to jump to clear high rocks, knows how to fly to shorten scary passages.

And I am learning to shut up and pedal in the strangest places, and I'm beginning to enjoy the view and the cool breeze on my face with my delightful constant companion, Jesus Christ.

And when I'm sure I just can't do any more, He just smiles and says, "Pedal." (Swindoll, *The Tale of the Tardy Oxcart*, 586–87)

What a great time to live! What exciting opportunities we have to prove our love for the Lord! Trust that he knows what he's doing. Lift up your head, look toward the horizon, and pedal.

Chapter 32

Children of Light

K ids are great. They're funny, playful, curious, and forgiving. My sons love Batman. They think he's the greatest superhero of all time. Michael runs around the house yelling, "I'm Batman." And my oldest son, Joseph, dresses up like Batman with mask, cape, bat utility belt, and everything else his favorite superhero needs. Every now and then the two of them get a little rough, and one of them gets hurt. They cry and carry on as if the world has come to an end. But after a few minutes, they forgive each other and get back to playing superhero.

One of the greatest ways we can prepare for the Second Coming is to become like children. Not in the sense of playing with dolls and action figures, although that could be a start, but in the sense of developing the Christlike qualities children have. After all, we're commanded to become like children. Submissiveness, meekness, humility, patience, and being loving are characteristics of children (Mosiah 3:19). As children of God, we should develop these qualities.

If you think about some of your favorite scripture stories, you'll realize that God seems to really like young people. Samuel the prophet was a young boy when the Lord spoke with him (1 Samuel 3). The two thousand stripling warriors were not very old but proved to be powerful warriors (Alma 53:18; 56:55–56; 58:39). Mormon was only fifteen when the Lord came to him (Mormon 1:15). Why did God protect or speak to these young men? Because they had childlike qualities. They had faith and were willing to obey and sacrifice.

In the Book of Abraham, in the Pearl of Great Price, we see a wonderful example of young people doing the Lord's will. Now keep in mind that at the beginning of the book of Abraham, the majority of the people were wicked, including the priests. One wicked priest even tried to kill Abraham, but he was spared by the Lord.

In the first chapter of Abraham, we learn about three other young people who tried to do what was right. They had developed the child-like quality of obedience. These three young people were sisters. They loved the Lord and wanted to do his will. We don't know much about them. We don't even know their names. But we do know that they were the daughters of a man named Onitah.

These three sisters were sacrificed on an altar by a wicked high priest. The scriptures tell us why. First, they were sacrificed because of their virtue. We can assume that their virtue was something that they refused to give up. The second reason is that they would not bow down and worship idols. They would only worship God (Abraham 1:11).

I can't imagine being one of those sisters. How would you like to have been the last one killed after watching the death of your beloved sisters? How easy would it have been for these sisters to just give in and give up all they had lived for? They could have, but they did not. The most important things to them were defending their faith, keeping their covenants, and doing the will of the Lord.

I look forward to meeting those sisters someday. I will thank them for their example. I have received strength in my life by looking to them and the courage they showed when times got rough. They were child-like, "willing to submit to all things which the Lord seeth fit to inflict upon [them], even as a child doth submit to his father" (Mosiah 3:19).

Children of light are those people who understand this principle. They do whatever the Lord asks of them. They do not say, "I'll do it my way." Rather, they say, "I'll do it God's way." These people are forgiving and loving. They defend their virtue and everything else that God values. They look to the prophet for guidance and counsel. They love their families and strive to bring harmony into their homes. They love their friends and help them by setting good examples for them. They love the Lord.

I remember a story about a young man who was having a hard time. He was a freshman in high school and didn't have many friends. One day when his depression had reached a peak, he decided to take his life. After school he gathered his books and emptied his locker, planning to not return the next day. On his way to the bus stop, he tripped and dropped his books. Feeling embarrassed, he began to pick them up.

A few yards away stood another young man. He was a popular foot-ball player who happened to see the incident. Quickly he knelt beside the boy and helped him pick up his books. He then asked if he could help him to the bus stop. Not much was said between the two other than "Thank you" and "You're welcome."

Three years passed, and graduation night came. Both of these young men were seniors. One of them was a successful football player and captain of the team; the other was a 4.0 student and the valedic-torian of the school. The young man who once wanted to take his life spoke that evening during graduation. He talked about the things he would miss and the challenges that lay ahead.

At the end of his speech, he told the story of a freshman who had decided to take his life and of a friend who had helped him with his books. He said that at that moment, while he was being helped, a thought crossed his mind: *Someone does care about me.* After he arrived home, he decided not to go through with his plans. The following day he took his books back to school. Addressing his friend, he said that if it hadn't been for his selfless service he wouldn't be speaking that evening.

Children of light do the Lord's will. They listen to the Spirit and obey. The Lord gives a special promise to those who qualify themselves to be children of light. He said, "And again, verily I say unto you, the coming of the Lord draweth nigh, and it overtaketh the world as a thief in the night—Therefore, gird up your loins, *that you may be the children of light, and that day shall not overtake you as a thief*" (D&C 106:4–5; emphasis added).

What an incredible promise. So what can you do today to become a child of light? Defend the truth as the daughters of Onitah did, and do the Lord's will. Look around. Maybe someone needs you today. Listen to the Holy Ghost and go find that person.

CHAPTER 33

How Will I Know If I'm Ready?

Of all the questions I receive as a teacher, the one I seem to be asked most is, "How will I know if I'm ready?" Most of us would like to know if we're ready. We want to be prepared for that great day when Christ comes out of heaven in a cloud of glory with his angels. I hope by the end of this chapter that you will be able to tell if you're ready. By the way, don't worry if you feel that you're the only one who has ever asked that question. Jesus' disciples asked a similar question.

"Tell us, when shall these things be?" they asked regarding the Lord's return. "And what shall be the sign of thy coming, and of the end of the world?" (Matthew 24:3). They focused their questions on Christ's return, but you can sense that they wanted to be ready for that day.

The scriptures teach us how to be ready. They present at least six different aspects of preparedness for the Second Coming. It would be a good idea to think about each one and see how you're doing in that area.

First, you'll be ready for the Second Coming if you're at peace. During King Benjamin's address his people had an amazing experience. They proclaimed that they had been given "peace of conscience"—a feeling that came because of their faith in Christ and their willingness to repent of their sins (Mosiah 4:3).

Have you ever felt that way? When we repent, the Spirit of the Lord can be with us, and it is the Spirit that gives us peace. Do you feel that way now? If you do, you're probably on track. You're repenting every day and striving to be worthy of the Spirit. If not, I know you can. It may not be easy, but you can repent today and have the peace you need to prepare for Christ's coming.

Elder Richard G. Scott said, "For a moment I speak to anyone who has succumbed to temptation. Please stop now. You can do it with help from an understanding parent, bishop, or stake president" ("The Power of Righteousness," *Ensign*, November 1998, 69). The peace that can come through repentance is worth the visit with loving parents and leaders.

Second, you will know if you're ready if you have joy. Alma asked an important question: "If ye have experienced a change of heart, and if ye have felt to sing the song of redeeming love, I would ask, can ye feel so now?" (Alma 5:26). What is it that helps us feel joy? It's obedience to the commandments of the Lord.

Lewis and Faye Copeland tell the story of a wild little boy who had to be hospitalized for several weeks:

> At a certain children's hospital, a boy gained a reputation for wreaking havoc with the nurses and staff. One day a visitor who knew about his terrorizing nature made him a deal: "If you are good for a week," she said, "I'll give you a dime when I come again." A week later she stood before his bed. "I'll tell you what,"

she said, "I won't ask the nurses if you behaved. You must tell me yourself. Do you deserve the dime?"

After a moment's pause, a small voice from among the sheets said: "Gimme a penny." (In Swindoll, *The Tale of the Tardy Oxcart*, 413)

Sometimes I wonder if we give the Lord a penny's worth of obedience rather than a dime's worth.

Third, you'll know if you're ready if you have no desire to do evil. The key word here is *desire*. All of us make mistakes and do wrong things. But is it our desire, every thought, motivation, and intent to do evil? I don't think so. I don't know too many people who lie awake at night thinking of wicked things to do. Most of us sin and make mistakes as part of mortality. We then repent and get back on track. King Benjamin's people said, "We have no more disposition to do evil, but to do good continually" (Mosiah 5:2). Our sincerest desires play a big part in preparing us for the Second Coming. "For where your treasure is, there will your heart be also" (Matthew 6:21).

Author Stephen E. Robinson wrote: "Through the atonement of Jesus Christ we can receive, despite our unworthiness, what we desire, what we long for—but only if it is what we really long for. So what do you want? What do you *really* want? . . . Blessed are they who desire with all their hearts to be righteous as Christ is righteous, to be perfect as he is perfect, who long for it and seek it, and who would give anything for it, though they do not have it. What is their reward? They shall, through the atonement of Christ, receive it according to their fondest desires!" (*Believing Christ*, 20).

Fourth, we'll be prepared if we have love for others. The hardest part of this one is loving people who don't seem to deserve our love—the guy who shoved me in the hall, the girl who made fun of my clothes, the date who left and went home without telling me before the dance was over, the little sister who sprayed my perfume all over the house. The Lord said, "A new commandment I give unto you, that ye love one another; as I have loved you, that ye also love one another" (John 13:34).

Fifth, you must have the image of God engraven upon your countenance (Alma 5:14). How do we do that? Alma tells us, "Therefore, if a man bringeth forth good works he hearkeneth unto the voice of the good shepherd, and he doth follow him" (Alma 5:41).

There are a lot of voices around us. We hear the voice of popularity, the voice of pride, the voice of wealth, and the voice of immorality. They cry out to us all the time. But remember, the voice we should listen to is the one that is much quieter than the others. If we listen to the still, small voice, we begin to change. Eventually, if we keep listening, we will become like the Lord.

"But charity is the pure love of Christ, and it endureth forever; and whoso is found possessed of it at the last day, it shall be well with him. . . . *When he shall appear we shall be like him,* for we shall see him as he is; that we may have this hope; that we may be purified even as he is pure" (Moroni 7:47–48; emphasis added).

Sixth, remember that you're not perfect. Some people believe that in order to be saved when Christ comes we have to be perfect. Perfection is a process that takes place as we change and repent. None of us will be perfect in this life. God has commanded us to be perfect, but he also understands that the process takes time (Matthew 5:48). If our desire focuses on repenting, improving, and serving others, we will be ready for Jesus to come.

Elder Neal A. Maxwell taught: "Our perfect Father does not expect us to be perfect children yet. He had only one such Child. Meanwhile, therefore, sometimes with smudges on our cheeks, dirt on our hands, and shoes untied, stammeringly but smilingly we present God with a dandelion—as if it were an orchid or a rose! If for now the dandelion is the best we have to offer, He receives it, knowing what we may later place on the altar. It is good to remember how young we are spiritually" (*Quote Book*, 243).

Knowing that you are ready for the Second Coming can come only from feelings you have within yourself. I know he wants you to be ready. So roll up your sleeves, put a smile on your face, and go to work!

CHAPTER 34

What Will It Be Like?

We often don't know what things will feel like or look like until they actually happen. Such is the case with the Second Coming. It's hard to tell what each of us will experience. I'm sure, depending on our preparation, that our experiences will vary. But we do have an idea of what we can expect, thanks to the Book of Mormon. The Book of Mormon was given as a guide to help us prepare for the day Christ comes. Studying the coming of Christ in the Book of Mormon may give us a glimpse into what it will be like for us.

When Christ came to the Americas, something interesting took place before he arrived. Our Father in Heaven introduced his Only Begotten Son, saying, "Behold my Beloved Son, in whom I am well pleased, in whom I have glorified my name—hear ye him" (3 Nephi 11:7). In the New Testament, the Father also introduced the Son. When John the Baptist baptized Jesus, the Father was likewise "well pleased" (Matthew 3:17). When the Prophet Joseph Smith had the

First Vision, the Father again introduced the Son (JS–H 1:17). Will the Father also introduce Jesus when he comes again? If he does, we may have the privilege of hearing the Father's voice. What a sweet experience that would be.

When Christ came to the land Bountiful, 2,500 people had gathered around the temple (3 Nephi 17:25). Read carefully what happened when he came: "And it came to pass that the Lord spake unto them saying: Arise and come forth unto me, that ye may thrust your hands into my side, and also that ye may feel the prints of the nails in my hands and in my feet, that ye may know that I am the God of Israel, and the God of the whole earth, and have been slain for the sins of the world.

"And it came to pass that the multitude went forth, and thrust their hands into his side, and did feel the prints of the nails in his hands and in his feet; and this they did do, going forth one by one until they had all gone forth, and did see with their eyes and did feel with their hands, and did know of a surety and did bear record, that it was he, of whom it was written by the prophets, that should come" (3 Nephi 11:13–15).

Can you image such an experience? Each of the 2,500 had the privilege of feeling the wounds in the Savior's hands and feet. This event may have taken all day. What does that tell us about the Savior? He wants each one of us to come to know him ourselves. He is aware of each one of us and wants us to prepare for the great day of his coming.

A few verses later we learn that the Lord commanded Nephi to come forth. "And Nephi arose and went forth, and bowed himself before the Lord and did kiss his feet" (3 Nephi 11:19).

Jesus then taught the people. At one point, when they were getting tired, he said he was going to go to the Father so they could rest. After telling them he would be back the next day, Jesus looked over the people and saw that they were in tears. They didn't want him to go. The next thing that happened teaches us much about the Savior.

"And he said unto them: Behold, my bowels are filled with compassion towards you. Have ye any that are sick among you? Bring them hither. Have ye any that are lame, or blind, or halt, or maimed, or leprous, or that are withered, or that are deaf, or that are afflicted in any manner? Bring them hither and I will heal them, for I have compassion upon you" (3 Nephi 17:6–7).

After healing the sick and afflicted, Jesus commanded that all the little children be brought to him. He asked the multitude to kneel on the ground, and then he began to pray. His prayer was so magnificent that it could not be written.

"And no tongue can speak, neither can there be written by any man, neither can the hearts of men conceive so great and marvelous things as we both saw and heard Jesus speak; and no one can conceive of the joy which filled our souls at the time we heard him pray for us unto the Father. And it came to pass that when Jesus had made an end of praying unto the Father, he arose; but so great was the joy of the multitude that they were overcome" (3 Nephi 17:17–18).

Because of the faith of the people, the Savior's joy was full, and he wept. Then he took their children, one by one, and blessed them and prayed for them. Then he wept again. Turning to the multitude, he said, "Behold your little ones." The record tells us that as the multitude "looked to behold they cast their eyes towards heaven, and they saw the heavens open, and they saw angels descending out of heaven as it were in the midst of fire; and they came down and encircled those little ones about, and they were encircled about with fire; and the angels did minister unto them" (3 Nephi 17:23–24).

For all of you who have felt like the girl in the first chapter, that there would be no hope for you during the Second Coming, I pray that you have found comfort in the words you have read. May your journey in the days ahead be one of joy, excitement, and preparation. I know there is hope for you, just as our prophet knows there is hope for you.

President Gordon B. Hinckley said:

> Let us go forward in this glorious work. How exciting and wonderful it is. I do not know how anybody can feel gloomy for very long who is a member of this Church. Do you feel gloomy? Lift your eyes. Stand on your feet. Say a few words of appreciation and love to the Lord. Be positive. Think of what great things are occurring as the Lord brings to pass His eternal purposes. . . . This is the day which has been spoken of by those who have gone before us. Let us live worthy of our birthright. Keep the faith. Nurture your testimonies. Walk in righteousness, and the Lord will bless you and prosper you and you will be a happy and wonderful people. (*Teachings of Gordon B. Hinckley*, 412–13)

I know that Jesus lives. I know he will come again. I know he will deliver the promised blessings that are reserved for the faithful. I know he loves you. Go forward with faith in the opportunities awaiting you in this life. Live every day as if it were the day of his coming. Look forward with hope and joy to that greatest of all events. Remember always what the Second Coming will be like.

It will be awesome!

SOURCES

Book of Mormon Student Manual. Salt Lake City: The Church of Jesus Christ of Latter-day Saints, 1982.

Cannon, George Q. *Gospel Truth.* 2 vols. in 1. Selected by Jerreld L. Newquist. Salt Lake City: Deseret Book, 1987.

Children's Songbook. Salt Lake City: The Church of Jesus Christ of Latter-day Saints, 1989.

Conference Reports of The Church of Jesus Christ of Latter-day Saints. Salt Lake City: The Church of Jesus Christ of Latter-day Saints, 1898 to present.

Dyer, Alvin R. *The Center Place of Zion.* Brigham Young University Speeches of the Year. 6 February 1967.

———. *The Refiner's Fire.* Salt Lake City: Deseret Book, 1960.

For the Strength of Youth: Fulfilling Our Duty to God. Salt Lake City: Intellectual Reserve, 2001.

Hinckley, Gordon B. *Lest We Forget.* Brigham Young University Speeches of the Year. 10 November 1970.

———. *Teachings of Gordon B. Hinckley.* Salt Lake City: Deseret Book, 1997.

Hunter, Howard W. *The Teachings of Howard W. Hunter.* Edited by Clyde J. Williams. Salt Lake City: Bookcraft, 1997.

Journal of Discourses, 26 vols. London: Latter-day Saints' Book Depot, 1854–86.

Kimball, Spencer W. *The Miracle of Forgiveness.* Salt Lake City: Bookcraft, 1969.

Lee, Harold B. "Born of the Spirit." Address to seminary and institute faculty. Brigham Young University, 26 June 1962.

———. "The Place of the Living Prophet, Seer, and Revelator." Address to seminary and institute faculty. Brigham Young University, 8 July 1964.

Ludlow, Daniel H. *A Companion to Your Study of the Book of Mormon.* Salt Lake City: Deseret Book, 1976.

Maxwell, Neal A. *The Neal A. Maxwell Quote Book.* Edited by Cory H. Maxwell. Salt Lake City: Bookcraft, 1997.

———. "Teaching by the Spirit—'The Language of Inspiration.'" In *Old Testament Symposium Speeches 1991.* Salt Lake City: The Church of Jesus Christ of Latter-day Saints, 1991.

McConkie, Bruce R. *A New Witness for the Articles of Faith.* Salt Lake City: Deseret Book, 1985.

———. *Doctrinal New Testament Commentary.* 3 vols. Salt Lake City: Bookcraft, 1965–73.

———. *The Millennial Messiah.* Salt Lake City: Deseret Book, 1982.

———. *Mormon Doctrine.* Salt Lake City: Bookcraft, 1966.

———. *The Promised Messiah.* Salt Lake City: Deseret Book, 1978.

Otten, Leaun G. and Max C. Caldwell. *Sacred Truths of the Doctrine and Covenants.* 2 vols. Springville, Utah: LEMB Inc., 1982–83.

Packer, Boyd K. *Teach Ye Diligently.* Salt Lake City: Deseret Book, 1975.

———. "To Those Who Teach in Troubled Times." In *Charge to Religious Educators.* 2d ed. Salt Lake City: The Church of Jesus Christ of Latter-day Saints, 1981.

Peterson, Mark E. *Joshua: Man of Faith.* Salt Lake City: Deseret Book, 1978.

Robinson, Stephen E. *Believing Christ.* Salt Lake City: Deseret Book, 1992.

Smith, Joseph. *History of The Church of Jesus Christ of Latter-day Saints.* Edited by B. H. Roberts. 2d ed. rev. 7 vols. Salt Lake City: The Church of Jesus Christ of Latter-day Saints, 1932–51.

———. *Teachings of the Prophet Joseph Smith.* Selected by Joseph Fielding Smith. Salt Lake City: Deseret Book, 1976.

Smith, Joseph Fielding. *Answers to Gospel Questions.* Compiled by Joseph Fielding Smith Jr. 5 vols. Salt Lake City: Deseret Book, 1957–66.

———. *Doctrines of Salvation.* Compiled by Bruce R. McConkie. 3 vols. Salt Lake City: Bookcraft, 1954–56.

———. *Signs of the Times.* Salt Lake City: Deseret Book, 1963.

———. *The Way to Perfection.* Salt Lake City: Deseret Book, 1975.

Swindoll, Charles R. *The Tale of the Tardy Oxcart and 1,501 Other Stories.* Nashville: Word Publishing, 1998.

Index